WHAT ARE THEY SAYING ABOUT
CHRIST AND WORLD RELIGIONS?

What Are They Saying About Christ And World Religions?

Lucien Richard, O.M.I.

PAULIST PRESS
New York/Ramsey

Acknowledgement
The Publisher gratefully acknowledges the use of 700 words from
JESUS: An Experiment in Christology by Edward Schillebeeckx. English translation copyright © 1979 by William Collins Sons & Co. Ltd., and The Seabury Press, Inc. Used by permission of The Crossroads Publishing Company.

Library of Congress
Catalog Card Number: 81-80878

ISBN: 0-8091-2391-6

Published by Paulist Press
545 Island Road, Ramsey, N.J. 07446

Printed and bound in the
United States of America

Contents

Introduction

Religious faith and religions have been defined as the quest for ultimate reality, for ultimate meaning. Because of this quest for ultimate reality, religions seem to have an inherent drive to claims of uniqueness and universality. There seems to be an inner tendency in various religions to claim to be *the* true religion, to offer *the* true revelation as *the* true way of salvation. It appears to be self-contradictory for a religion to accept an expression of ultimate reality other than its own.

Yet what characterizes the contemporary scene is religious pluralism. While it is true that the world has always been religiously plural, we are experiencing today a qualitatively different kind of pluralism from the past. This difference is evident in the fact of an accepted pluralistic attitude of mind that questions the claims to universality and absoluteness of every form of religious belief, not only from outside the religious belief but also from within. For the pluralistic mind all religions and world views are historically conditioned, relative to various stages of historical development and as such cannot claim ultimate allegiance, nor promise an ultimate truth nor an ultimate salvation. In a pluralistic perspective, no particular religion can ever be the unique and only religion of mankind.

The drive to claims of uniqueness and universality is particularly true of monotheistic religions and especially of Christianity. Christianity proclaims Jesus Christ as the one mediator without whom there is no salvation. In him God united itself in unreserved intimacy bridging the abyss of human and divine difference. At a particular place and time in a series of specific historical events, the Christ event, the relationships between God and humanity have been changed in an absolute and decisive way. What is characteristic of Christianity's understanding about God is that while it sees God as effectively related to all creation, he is nevertheless known most clearly and decisively in certain places and through certain events and persons. In this perspective very little theological space is left for other religions; a confrontation with the contemporary pluralistic mind becomes extremely problematic and dangerous.

It has become apparent to many Christians that the contemporary pluralistic mind must be confronted and that other religious traditions can no longer be viewed in a negative or condescending way. These religions are recognized as having their own integrity and impressive achievement. In their vitality they refuse to be disqualified by Christianity's claim to be the one and true way to God. The very fact of this vitality poses a challenge to Christianity. There was a time when Christians could believe that all they needed to convert all men and women to Jesus Christ was more missionaries and more resources. Today it is clearly apparent that that cannot be the case: there is no part of the world where the extra-Christian religions[1] appear to be moribund. The Moslem, Hindu and Buddhist traditions have remained intact and vital. Does this fact contradict God's plans or Christianity's claims? Or is it the fact that, God's salvific will being universal, its effects should be experienced and evident within the concrete order and not outside human history?

The body of literature resulting from the encounter of religions has gained clarity and focus in recent years. The question of other religions has emerged as an important dimension of contemporary Christian theology. Many theologians have concluded that theology cannot continue to be made in isolation from an interior dialogue with other religious traditions, that in fact the future of Christian theology lies in the deepest possible assimilation of the spirit and findings of other religions.[2] The data from non-Christian religions has become an essential element for theological reflection, which has to grapple with the existence and value of other religions and to account theologically for religious pluralism.

Theology has to come out of a faith experience, where other religions in the world are actually questions posed and possibilities offered to every believer. Other religious traditions have become part of the theologian's existential situation. He may experience them, not simply on a theoretical level, but in the concrete as realities which put the absolute claim of his own Christian faith in question.

The Task of Theology

Certain theologians have defined the task of theology from within the framework of the encounter with world religions. According to R. Whitson, the work of theology is to open one's religious tradition to another, both theologically and experientially.[3] The other religious tradition is to be perceived from within one's own tradition, one's own commitment.[4] A type of cross-fertilization must take place where the spiritual wisdom and experience of another's religion affects one's own religious outlook.

The major obstacle to this perception of the task of theology remains Christianity's claim to uniqueness and normativeness. This claim has essential ties with several fundamental doctrines: the doctrine of salvation and the history of salvation, the doctrine of revelation and, most basically, Christology.[5] The questions that need to be asked if theology is to be carried out in the broad ecumenical perspective outlined above are basically Christological. Can Christianity accept other religious traditions as valid ways to salvation without giving up its fundamental conviction about the absoluteness and uniqueness of Jesus Christ?[6] Is it possible to believe simultaneously that God has acted decisively and for the salvation of all in the person of Jesus Christ and that Jews, Hindus, Muslims and Buddhists are warranted in remaining who they are and in following their own different ways to salvation?

It has been claimed that Christology cannot accept other religions as avenues of salvation as long as it remains committed to the Christology contained in its official teaching.[7] Since Nicea and Chalcedon, Christology has made Christianity one of the world's great exclusivist religions. In this perspective, claims of uniqueness and universality about Jesus have been anchored over the centuries in the doctrine of the hypostatic unity as defined at Chalcedon. M. Wiles describes this understanding in the following way: ". . .that Jesus of Nazareth is unique in the precise sense that while being fully man, it is true of him and of him alone that he is also fully God, the second person of the co-equal Trinity."[8] The incarnation is here understood as a unique and distinctive identification of God's Logos with Jesus.

This understanding of the doctrine of the incarnation has come under serious questioning in recent years.[9] Such a questioning would seem to present a radical challenge to the claims about Jesus' uniqueness and finality. As D.N. Nineham wrote:

> . . . shall the Christian myth or story of the future be a story primarily about God or shall it, if I may put it so without irreverence, be a story which co-stars Jesus and God? Shall it be a story in which Jesus shares the leading role and has a unique or perfect status of some sort assigned to him? Or shall it be a story in which the protagonist's role belongs undividedly to God, though of course the story would tell how once he worked in a vitally important way—though not a way *necessarily* in principle unique—through the man Jesus to bring the Christian people into a relationship of reconciliation and oneness with himself?[10]

The Universality of Christ in the New Testament

Yet it is quite evident that the claims of finality and uniqueness made for Jesus Christ arise formally from the place assigned to Jesus in the New Testament. A survey of the New Testament makes it clear that Christianity's claims to Jesus' uniqueness and finality have other roots than the doctrine of the incarnation.

There is evidence in the New Testament of a momentum and directionality at work in the scope of the New Testament witness to Jesus as the Christ: from doxological affirmations taken from the language expressive of the hope of Israel to the universal affirmation of Colossians.

What takes place in the life and death of Jesus of Nazareth, together with the occurrences after his death which brought the disciples to belief in the resurrection formed a complex historical event, the Christ event, which was placed by the early Christians in the context of Israel's paradigmatic history. Inherent to Israel's history was the consciousness of being the chosen people. With Abraham a new race (Gen. 12:1–2) was constituted and with the exodus a new people was created (Dt. 4:35–40), "the people of Yahweh." Israel is a people different from other people, "for you are a people consecrated to Yahweh your God; it is you that Yahweh your God has chosen to be his very own people" (Dt. 7:6). It is a people with a mission: "Every knee shall bend before Yahweh, every tongue shall swear by him" (Is. 45:23). In fact at the time of Jesus we find an unparalleled period of missionary activity for Israel.[11] In Romans 2:17–23 Paul describes how the unshakable certainty of the Jewish people that they possessed the true and absolute revelation of God found expression in a sense of duty incumbent upon them to make this revelation known to the pagans.

Although the New Testament relates that Jesus forbade his disciples during his lifetime to preach to non-Jews: "Go not to the Gentiles and enter not the province of Samaria but go rather to the lost sheep of the house of Israel" (Mt. 10:15), we find the disciples involved in intensive missionary work very soon after the resurrection. In light of the resurrection the early Church saw Jesus as the embodiment of all of God's promises brought to fruition, and the Christ event as the realization of revelation and history. They gave this event both a universal and a final importance. The initial community of faith understood itself as the new chosen people, the people of a new covenant, the "first fruits" of what was to be. What had happened to them in their little history was more symbolic of the purposes of God in and for all creation. For them Jesus fulfilled the promises of the Old Testament: he was the fulfillment of God's saving purposes. As Paul wrote: "When anyone is united to Christ, there is a new act of creation; the old order has gone, and a new order has already begun" (2 Cor. 5:17).

The New Testament tells us that in Jesus Christ the time is fulfilled (Mk. 1:15), the fullness of time has arrived (Gal. 4:4), and the Scripture has been fulfilled (Lk. 4:21). In Jesus Christ, God accomplished and fulfilled the promise made to Abraham for all the people of the world (Lk. 1:55, 73). Jesus Christ is presented as the one who sums up and fulfills in his own person the whole history of the people of Israel. The covenant established by God with creation, with Israel, becomes focused in the one person of Jesus Christ. "And there is salvation in no one else, for there is no other name under heaven given among men by which we must be saved" (Acts 4:12). Jesus' existence and words are understood as disclosive of God. This is expressed by John as the enfleshing of the eternal Logos, the one who created the world.

Paul and the Universal Lordship of Christ

Paul attributes a universal Lordship to Jesus Christ. How seriously this definitive Lordship of Christ is taken becomes especially clear in the fifth chapter of Romans. Here we find the on-going repetition that just as there has been one Adam, so there is one second Adam. His coming means a complete change in the situation of mankind in that he brings new life and a new and final phase of history. Adam is the prototype who foreshadows Jesus Christ because Adam is the father of the old humanity as Jesus Christ is the father of the new humanity.[12] Paul sees Jesus' significance grounded in the fact that in him the final eschatological destiny of humanity has already appeared (Rom. 8:29).

He dominates all the centuries and sums up all creatures in himself. "He is the image of the unseen God and the first-born of all creation, for in him were created all things" (Col. 1:15). The supreme exaltation outlined in Colossians implies a universal active presence throughout creation and in the whole of human history. God's sending of his Son in the world is a unique and decisive act of salvation. It is wholly new, but it is in continuity with God's relationship with Israel and works its fulfillment.

What emerges out of the New Testament are two different strands of thought that serve as groundings for claims about uniqueness and finality. The universalism of the New Testament has its source and foundation in the one person of Jesus Christ as God's very special agent and ultimate fulfillment of God's promises. The doctrine of the incarnation is an attempt to express Jesus Christ's special agency. The doctrine of pre-existence and the title of Logos provided a foundation for a doctrine which attributed all the manifestations of pagan wisdom to Christ as the pre-existent and eternal Logos. Here lies the possibility of a Christian universalism that would see the work of Christ in all religions. The doctrine of the Trinity arose precisely because of the magnitude of the Christian community's claim about Christ. The other affirmation of the New Testament about Jesus Christ is that in him sacred history has already come to its end. Realized eschatology is one of the roots for the Church's claims about Jesus Christ's uniqueness and finality.[13] The doctrine of the uniqueness and finality of Jesus Christ is grounded in the concepts of incarnation and realized eschatology. Both concepts are seen by contemporary theologians as problematic to a genuine Christian openness. Both concepts lead to the absolutization and the freezing of attention on one human being and one moment in time.

The contemporary opposition to classical Christology and the doctrine of the incarnation, while constituting a clear challenge to the doctrine of uniqueness and finality of Christ, does not eliminate the grounds for this doctrine. The grounds are found in the New Testament. A realistic ecumenical approach to theology cannot simply be content with a few marginal correctives. It must examine the very center and authority of its proclamation, the New Testament. Is it possible to purify the Christian message of its claims without invalidating the message altogether? The question becomes one about Christian identity, and Jesus Christ is fundamental to that identity. At the center of an ecumenical approach to theology lies the question of Christology.

This book is about Christology as its affects Christianity's view of other world religions. It is about the ways in which the fundamental challenge of world religions to traditional Christology is understood and dealt with. It focuses on certain seminal contributions and attempts to span denominational lines.

The first chapter begins with several Protestant positions. The second chapter identifies and discusses several Catholic positions. The third chapter indicates points of convergence and differences and basic questions that still need to be dealt with. The conclusion indicates certain possible directions for future development.

1
Protestant Positions

Catholic and Protestant theologians are contributing to the Christology now emerging out of a faith experience which has taken seriously the vital existence of other religious traditions. These contemporary contributions, however, are not without preparation and antecedents. In examining contemporary Christologies, Hegel's continued relevance becomes apparent,[14] and his focus on the question of the relationship between the historical, individual Jesus of Nazareth and the absolute-truth claims made in reference to the Christ of faith is still the basic question for twentieth-century theologians.[15] One of Hegel's major theological interests concerned the connections between Christ and the course of the historical process; for Hegel, the Christian symbols provide a comprehensive interpretation of the whole scope of historical development. There is no attempt on Hegel's part "to provide a secure shelter for religious truth outside of space and time,"[16] and there is no final end for created reality that is not in continuity with the present. Hegel emphasizes the intimate relation between culture and religion. In affirming Christ as the supreme appearance of the unity between man and God, Hegel advocated a universal dimension to Christianity which jeopardized the Jesus of history.

1. Nineteenth-Century Background

The most lucid expression of the Christological debate following Hegel is to be found in David Friedrich Strauss' book, *The Life of*

Jesus Critically Examined.[17] Strauss argued that certainty about the truth of Christianity is not dependent upon historical knowledge of facts. He could not accept that the hypostatic unity existed in a single, historical individual, and he offered his position in the form of rhetorical questions. "And is this no true realization of the idea? Is not the idea of a unity of the divine and human natures a real one in a far higher sense, when I regard the whole scene of mankind as its realization, than when I single out one man as such a realization? Is not an incarnation of God from eternity a truer one than an incarnation limited to a particular point in time?"[18] The division of the Christ principle from the historical Jesus was accompanied by a steep skepticism about the historical reliability of the Gospels. F. Schleiermacher had already rejected the metaphysical and ontological aspects of Chalcedon and had approached the interpretation of the meaning of Christ from the side of his manhood, inaugurating the modern humanistic approach to Christology. He accepted as a fact universal religious consciousness which he understood as formally a feeling of absolute dependence. He grounded the Christian faith in the more universal human phenomenon of religious experience and not simply in authoritative sources. This was a turning inward to subjective insights and away from outward authority.[19] While Christianity is understood by Schleiermacher as the highest form of religion, other religions are understood as positive expressions of the same universal religious consciousness. According to John Macquarrie, "It would be difficult to think of another century in the history of Christian theology when the structure of orthodoxy was subjected to such a series of shocks as beat upon it in these works."[20] The orthodoxy that followed Schleiermacher was either a development or a refutation of his position. He initiated a Copernican revolution in theology and in Christology.

While these theological giants generally had a rather superficial knowledge of other religious traditions, they did attempt to deal with the problem of Christianity's exclusivism. These theologians established the theological climate for the past hundred years, and their thought is best expressed in Ernest Troeltsch's position of religious relativism. Yet as we survey the contemporary Protestant scene it comes as a surprise to discover that much of Protestant thought since the First World War, instead of building on the liberal understanding of religion, has reinforced the traditional Christian exclusivism. The reason for this is that the liberal position was radically opposed by Karl Barth. Troeltsch and Barth were diametrically opposed: they present the opposing poles of the spectrum: relativism and absolutism, exclusivism and universalism. Troeltsch (1865–1923), a catalyst for the Protestant theology of religion, was the systematic theologian for the "Religionsgeschichliche Schule," the school of comparative religion, founded by H. Günkel and W. Bousset.[21] This group of scholars underlined the dependence of the Old Testament and New Testament on their religious environment. They demanded a revision of the established ideas on the nature and origin of Christianity as a religion, a revision which implied an interdependence between Christianity and other religions.

Troeltsch and the Relativizing of Christianity

Troeltsch's basic approach was history as understood and proposed in the writings of W. Dilthey. Everything that human reality is and produces is historical and is subject to the law of historical development. Troeltsch moved away from a supernaturalistic understanding of the origin of religion including Christianity. He understood history in an evolutionary perspective. There is a universal movement toward perfection which means that the end can never be fully grasped along the evolutionary process. Everything in some way is related, and Christianity and theology must be opened to relativism. This excludes all absolutism. Revelation as part of history is in a progressive movement toward the Absolute, but it can never attain it. God's revelations in the Old Testament and in Jesus Christ, as unique and special as they may be, are only stages in the general history of revelation.

In his essay on the significance of the historicity of Jesus for Christian faith,[22] Troeltsch understood Jesus' centrality simply as fulfilling the necessary requirements for the development of any tradition. "Decisive for the appraisal of the significance of Jesus is, therefore, not the unavailability of salvation for non-Christians but rather the need of the religious community for a support, a center, and a symbol of its religious life."[23] Jesus Christ is the means by which we grasp the essence of religiosity, which Troeltsch considers to be personalism. But Jesus Christ cannot be identified with the essence: that is above him and beyond him. Jesus Christ must take his place—not an essentially different place—among the other founders of great religions.

Troeltsch saw Christianity as historically relative and conditioned as any other tradition. "In all moments of its history Christianity is a purely historical phenomenon just like the other great religions."[24] One may not claim absolute validity for Christianity; the "criteria of its validity" can only be "the evidence of a profound inner experience."[25] Claims of absoluteness and uniqueness for any tradition can only be made on the basis of a personal conviction or confession. Truth is always truth for me, for my culture, for my religion. Christianity can no longer be termed the point of "convergence" or the goal of the history of religion; it is simply a special form of religion. In dealing with Christianity's claim to the uniqueness and finality of Christ within the context of its own historical particularity, Troeltsch argued for a provisional pluralism and a better appreciation of other religious traditions.[26]

2. Karl Barth and Christomonism

Troeltsch's position on the uniqueness of Jesus Christ and Christianity was radically opposed by Karl Barth and by his followers. Fundamental to Barth's position is a clear distinction between revelation which is understood as divine action, and religion which is simply a human activity. Barth's understanding of Christ, which has been labeled Christomonism is the starting point and foundation of his evaluation of other religions. It is Barth's contention that revelation has become a reality in Christ and nowhere else. This is clearly affirmed at the beginning of the second half-volume of *Church Dogmatics.* "According to the Holy Scripture God's revelation takes place in that God's Word becomes a man, in that this man was God's Word. The Incarnation of the eternal Word, Jesus Christ is God's revelation."[27] All attempts on the part of men and women to know God outside of Jesus Christ are useless. God's activity in Christ absorbs and in a sense negates all human activity. Man can

know nothing about God except what God has revealed about himself—there are no innate capacities. Men and women have no innate
capacities to experience the divine; all capacities are given to them
by the Word itself. Religion is perceived by Barth as man's attempt
to do what only Christ can do: reveal and please God.[28] As such, religion and religions are totally opposed to Christ and his revelation.[29]

Religion for Barth is *unglaube,* lack of faith. Revelation in
Christ is for Barth the abolition of religion, which is in fact the title
of the section in *Church Dogmatics* that deals with this question.

To give extra-Christian religion a theological meaning is to be-
tray the unique role of Christ. Without Christ, Christianity is like all
other religions. Christianity is unique because it is justified in Jesus
Christ; this justification in no way implies "an immanent content of
truth."[30] The analogy of the sun illuminating the earth is a useful
way of understanding Barth's concept of religions and Christianity.
Like the sun, Christ's light falls on one part of the earth and not on
the other, enlightening one part and leaving the other in darkness,
and this without ever changing the religion itself. All depends on the
light of Christ shining here and not there on the "act of divine elec-
tion." The only difference between Christianity and other religions
is that Christianity stands in the sunlight, the others in the shadows.

Barth's position on religions is rooted in his Christology, which
is focused on the incarnation. He writes of revelation in terms of the
person of Jesus Christ. The uniqueness of Christ's revelation for us
is "the analogue of what God is in his being antecedently in himself,
the Son of the Father beside whom there can as little be a second,
as there can be a second God alongside of the one God."[31] In other
words: "We have to take revelation so utterly seriously that in it as
the act of God we have to recognize immediately his being as well."[32]

Karl Barth's appraisal of extra-Christian religions had a predominant and lasting influence on Protestant theology. From Christ
the center, Protestant theology sought to understand the value and
nature of religions. In this search the biblical message does not in any
way represent man's search for the transcendent but God's free and
unilateral approach to us. For Barth the humanity of Jesus Christ
simply mirrors the divine. Even in the incarnation the gulf between
the human and the divine still exists. The revelation of God in Jesus
Christ, so to speak, bounces off the surface of the world in the way

that a beam of light is reflected from a mirror in a flash of brilliance without affecting the mirror.

3. W. Pannenberg and Universal History

Contemporary Protestant theologians have attempted to avoid the relativism of Troeltsch and the exclusivism of Barth. One such theologian is Wolfhart Pannenberg. Pannenberg's purpose is to revise the idea of a Christian understanding of universal history, within which the history of Christianity is closely related to the history of other religions. In the past, either Jesus Christ was dogmatically imposed as the absolute norm of other religions, or the revelation in Jesus was lost in a general set of truths to be found more or less fully in all historical religions. Pannenberg attempts to integrate Jesus' revelation within the history of other religions without depriving it of normative significance. The revelation in Jesus should not be seen as an isolated event whose meaning is accessible only to the faithful. Revelation in Jesus Christ must occur and is understandable only in the religio-historical process and context. Pannenberg writes: "Only through Jesus does it become clear what the God of Israel really is and means. And yet this final understanding presupposes a knowledge of this God prior to it and also a hope for God's presence."[33] Any revelation must take place in a religio-historical context and must be approached as such. A positive dialogue between Christianity and the other religions is necessary. This dialogue is founded on the universal meaning of the historical process.

Pannenberg affirms God's presence through revelation in other religious traditions. The foundation for this presence is the existential structure of human reality and the nature of the historical process. Anthropology and history are important keys in understanding Pannenberg's theology of history.

A human being is a questioning being in constant search for answers that lie beyond a particular existence and history.[34] It is a questioning that can be expressed and experienced only within history. Yet the discovery of reality in its unity and totality can only be discovered at the end of history. What can be experienced now is simply a prophetic movement toward final unity.

Man's questioning, searching and the possibility of discovering unity occur primarily within the religious and therefore within the historical process. The presence of God within historical religions is a form of universal divine revelation. And the reality of Jesus as revealer must be understood from within this context of historical religions.

> Jesus of Nazareth is the final revelation of God because the end of history appeared in him. It did so both in his eschatological message and in his resurrection from the dead. However he can be understood to be God's final revelation only in connection with the whole of history as mediated by the history of Israel. He is God's revelation in the fact that all history receives its light from him.[35]

The Inductive Approach

Pannenberg's approach to Christology, dictated by his understanding of history, is inductive. It lays great emphasis upon the objective historicity of Jesus as the ground of faith. "Christology is concerned, therefore, not only with unfolding the Christian community's confession in Christ, but above all with grounding it in the activity and fate of Jesus in the past."[36] The starting point of his Christology is Jesus in himself. What is important is the significance of Jesus "in himself, in his history, and in his person constituted by this history."[37] For Pannenberg, Christological questions are best approached "by Christologies from below to above" and not "Christologies from above to below."[38] Christology must substantiate the Church's claims about Christ. To do this, the movement must be from the historical Jesus to the recognition of his divinity; the incarnation emerges as a conclusion.[39]

The divinity of the man Jesus can only be substantiated in light of the resurrection. "As this man, as man in this particular, unique situation with this particular historical mission and this particular fate, Jesus is not just man, but, from the perspective of his resurrection from the dead, he is one with God and thus is himself God."[40] In light of the resurrection Pannenberg understands Christ as the one in whom God reveals the end and in whom God brings men and women to salvation. "In the destiny of Jesus the end of all history has happened in advance as prolepsis."[41]

With other prevalent theologians, Pannenberg holds to the finality of Jesus Christ and his revelation. Christ brings a final revelation insofar as he proleptically contains the end of all history which is the origin and driving force and end of all religion. ". . . in the fate of Jesus, the end of history is experienced in advance versus an anticipation,"[42] and in "the fate of Jesus as the anticipation of the end of all history, God is revealed as the one God of all mankind who had been expected since the times of the prophets."[43] The Christ-event is an event for all peoples, since in Christ "God is finally and fully revealed,"[44] and "no further revelation of God can happen."[45]

Pannenberg's approach to Christology claims to be inductive. He turns to experience as the ground for any affirmation on the relative value of different religions in comparison to Christianity. "As long as the whole of reality can be understood more deeply and more convincingly through Jesus than without him, it proves true in our everyday experience and personal knowledge that in Jesus the creative origin of all reality stands revealed."[46]

Yet the centrality and universality of Jesus as an historical figure cannot be arrived at simply from a below approach. Pannenberg must have recourse to the reality of the future, to eschatology. The conclusive proof of Jesus' finality can only be given at the end.

Two questions arise relative to Pannenberg's appreciation of extra-Christian religions. The first question is: How can the finality and uniqueness of any tradition, and in this case of Christianity, be established inductively? Implied in the choice of an inductive method is a deliberate empirical attitude, unwilling to impose closure on the quest for truth, and in this case for religious truth, by invoking any authority whatever.

Yet, as written above, when Pannenberg affirms the universality of Jesus, he must have recourse to eschatology. The uniqueness of Jesus of Nazareth and his objective universal Lordship are based on the fact that his mission and message are authenticated by the resurrection. The resurrection also makes possible the identification of Jesus of Nazareth with God's Son.

The resurrection is understood by Pannenberg as a literal appearance of the absolute in history that takes up history in a process that leads to the kingdom. Jesus' resurrection has inaugurated an historical process that leads to the kingdom of God. Yet as an eschatological event, the resurrection is beyond the grasp of any inductive method. It can only be accepted on the authority of faith. Only faith can claim that God has been decisively and cosmically revealed in Jesus Christ.

The other question that can be asked of Pannenberg is whether believers in other religious traditions can find salvation in and through their religions. Does the God of Jesus Christ reveal himself through historical religions as the God who saves?

For Pannenberg revelation and salvation are identical; both imply God as present. But God is present proleptically and this only in Jesus Christ. Christ's finality places him both within and beyond the history of religions. In a sense, non-Christian religions cannot break out of their questionableness; they cannot know God sufficiently to receive the salvation effected in Christ. Although God is experienced in other religions, he is not really known. And therefore he does not really save.

Pannenberg's reservations on the salvific value of other religious traditions do not stem from his understanding of justification or from the *solo Christo* of the tradition. Yet they have their foundation in his Christology, in his understanding of Jesus Christ as the historically limited prolepsis in which God reveals the end. Pannenberg has not been able to bring about a middle of the road approach, a concept of Christianity which would bring out clearly its fundamental distinctions from other religions and yet show that this distinction does not set Christianity completely above other traditions. Cannot God in his universal salvific will make us aware of other salvific mediations besides that of the humanity of Jesus? Must the encounter with God's love which is a salvific encounter be necessarily related to Jesus of Nazareth? It appears that Pannenberg has given a negative answer to these questions and in doing so is following the traditional Protestant position.

4. The World Council of Churches and Cosmic Christology

A different approach to these questions has originated in the World Council of Churches, under the name of cosmic Christology.[47]

The emphasis is on the mystery of the incarnation in its revealing and saving force for the total creation. The cosmic Christ is present to every aspect of human history and of human endeavor. He brings about a new creation, and as such he is not only the head of the Church but of the total humanity. He is present in all religious traditions and must be discovered there.

This cosmological view of Christ is one of the oldest approaches in Christology. The first apologist, Justin Martyr, applies the Stoic concept of *Logos spermaticos* to justify his universal claims for the Logos, Jesus Christ. Justin's view becomes one of the principal ways of approach of the Apostolic Fathers to try to formulate a theological view of the relation of the Christian faith to the non-Christian religions. It affords the possibility of combining the claim of uniqueness and finality for Christ with a full recognition of the valid elements in other religions.

5. John Cobb and Logos Christology

John Cobb, a Protestant American theologian, has given a systematic foundation to this approach. John Cobb's basic approach in his book, *Christ in a Pluralistic Age,* is that the process of transformation needed for theology to be open to all religious traditions can be identified as "Christ," for, according to Cobb, Christ is the Way that excluded no ways. Cobb is asking for a transference of commitment from "every form in which Christ has previously been known to the process of creative transformation that is the reality of Christ itself."[49] Cobb sees the various religious traditions as claims and opportunities for Christian theology and the context in which Christ must be reconceived.[50] In fact, much that was meant by Christ in the past, when we did not acknowledge pluralism, becomes destructive in our new situation. The universalizing and absolutizing of Christianity's claim relative to Christ's work "is in opposition to our real need today."[51] According to Cobb:

> . . .[it is] precisely through deepening its central conviction of incarnation that Christian faith moves toward its own transformation through openness to all faiths. The creative

tranformation of theology that leads toward universality
can responsibly be identified as Christ.[52]

A positive appreciation of pluralism is a necessary correlate of
any authentic Christology. Faithfulness to Christ requires immersion
in a pluralistic consciousness,[53] because Christ breaks the relation to
himself as objectified figure and becomes the principle of liberation
at work in theology itself.[54] Every sacred form must be relativized,
and that process is in fact itself Christ.[55] Both Pannenberg and
Whitehead seem to play an essential role in Cobb's evolution from
Jesuology to Christology. These influences can be seen in relation to
his doctrine of faith and reason and of self and person. Cobb does
not see faith as a source of special knowledge.[56] The correlation of
faith and the sacred must be broken, and the relativizing consequences
of such a break have to be fully accepted by the Christian. No longer
is it necessary to choose between theology on the one side and the
objective study of religion as a phenomenon on the other.[57] This understanding of faith and reason leads to a reappraisal of classical
Christology. Cobb wants to affirm literally and seriously the incarnation of the Logos, but without the supernaturalist or exclusive implications of traditional theology.

Self and Person

Cobb's reappraisal of classical Christology involves a Whiteheadian understanding of self and person.[58] While Whitehead does
not see the person as the total human organism, but the psyche,
Cobb does not identify the self even with the psyche but only with
one element within it. The self is that "relatively continuous center
within human experience around which the experience attempts
more or less successfully to organize itself."[59] Selfhood is constituted
when the "I" transcends the affective and rational dimension of the
psyche. Cobb is advocating a complete rejection of any substantialist
categories relative to the self and the person. Selves conceived as substances can act upon each other only externally, and there is always
an inherently negative element in being acted upon in this way. In
substances, only accidents or attributes change; substances remain

identical; they can only relate to one another externally, while experiences can be genuinely present to one another.[60] Self-identity does not need to be explained by a numerical identity uniting past, present, and future experience.

Logos and Incarnation

The incarnation or the immanence of a transcendent reality cannot be understood in a substantialist context. The transcendent reality here is the Logos, "the cosmic principle of order, the ground of meaning and the source of purpose."[61] The Logos is fully incarnated when it constitutes not only a necessary aspect of existence, but the self as such.[62] The Logos is identical with the center or principles in terms of which other elements in experience are ordered. The incarnation means: a human "I" fulfilled through its identity with the immanent Logos. There is no confrontation of an "I" by a "Thou," for the Logos does not come from outside the "I," nor is self-identity lost by identifying with the Logos but perfected thereby.

While the Logos is incarnate in all human beings, Jesus is a paradigm case of incarnation. Cobb speaks of Jesus as the "perfect" and "normative" incarnation. The Logos not only constitutes a necessary dimension of his existence, but Jesus' self as such. "In Jesus there is a distinctive incarnation because his very selfhood was constituted by the Logos."[63] Cobb sees here the difference of Jesus' selfhood from that of all others. In Jesus, the Logos was normatively incarnate, and that incarnation "was not simply an intensification of the presence of the Logos in all people. It was a distinctive structure of existence in which Jesus' selfhood was co-constituted by the incarnation of the Logos; that is to say, Jesus was Christ."[64] The distinctiveness of Jesus can be spoken of in terms of Christ. Christ is the incarnate Logos. As such, Christ is present in all things. The degree and the kind of Christ's presence varies. The fullest form of that presence is that in which he co-constitutes with the personal past the very selfhood of a person. In that case, Christ is not simply present in a person but he is that person. Cobb sees the special presence of God in Jesus in that way. Christ does not designate Jesus as such, but refers to Jesus in a particular way, namely, as the incarnation of the divine. It does not designate deity as such but refers to deity experienced as graciously incarnate in the world.[65]

For Christians, then, Christ names what is supremely important, and as such is found in Jesus. "Those who experienced what is supremely important as bound up with Jesus are Christians."[66] But that recognition is not simply passive; it implies a creative transformation. Christ has to be realized in each and every one. "If the content of our hope is Christ, then it is the hope that Christ be perfectly formed in us."[67] Our goal is the structure of existence already realized in Jesus. "The fulfillment of this movement in the co-constitution by our personal past, and the Logos would be that perfection of incarnation already attained in Jesus."[68]

Within a processive framework, Cobb has revived the Logos Christology. While the Logos has always been operative in human history and is still operating, it is still important to recognize and name him. Christians know in naming the Logos "Christ" that the Divine has constituted itself toward the world as Love, and that love is creative transformation.

Cobb has insisted that any understanding of Christ must be grounded in the historical Jesus. He argues that it is possible to know enough about the historical Jesus to assert that he himself claimed a unique authority for his words and implicity affirmed that his actions were "directly expressive of God's purposes."[69] But what must be established is not simply what Jesus claimed but whether that claim is authentic. History cannot be appealed to in order to establish such a claim. It becomes clear how difficult it is to have a Christology in a "from below" approach. The basic thrust of a Logos Christology is that the subject of Christological affirmations, such as uniqueness and finality, is not the historical Jesus. The Logos Christology is always in danger of losing its grasp upon the decisiveness of the concrete particularity of the event.

6. Shubert Ogden and Existential Christology

Certain implications of the Logos Christology are found in the thought of Shubert Ogden who has characterized Christianity's claim to uniqueness and its christocentric exclusivism as mythological.[70] Myth is taken as expressing an existential self-understanding, an understanding of one's existence in its constant structure and in relation to its ultimate ground and end. The point of Christology for Ogden is strictly existential. "The only meaning that the event Jesus Christ has is a purely existential meaning."[71] To believe in Jesus Christ and to understand oneself authentically are one and the same thing. Contrary to Bultmann, Ogden claims that authentic human existence is possible in fact, not only in Jesus, but elsewhere. The word spoken in Jesus is addressed to all.[72]

The content of this possibility is man's ontological possibility of authentic historical existence before God.[73] This ontological possibility of authentic human existence leads Ogden to universalize the Christ dimension of Jesus. Jesus' life, his historical existence, became a "witness to the truth that all things have their ultimate beginning and solely in God's pure unbounded love, and that it is in giving ourselves wholly into the keeping of that love, by surrendering all other securities, that we realize authentic life."[74]

The life of Jesus is significant because it confronts us with the possibility of self-understanding. What is of major importance here is not the past event of what occurred between Jesus and God, but the present event that occurs between us and God through our encounter with the Christian witness to Jesus as the Christ. Ogden refuses to say that Jesus realized in his person complete authentic existence.

The office of Christ is that of being the bearer of God's eternal Word.[75] Jesus is Christ because he re-presents the possibilities of faith and for Christians, re-presents it decisively. In Jesus' word and deed, the ultimate truth about human life before God can be understood.[76] There is a normative dimension to this re-presentation in Jesus, for "in distinction from all other historical events, the ultimate truth about our existence before God is normatively represented as revealed."[77]

For Ogden, the concept of re-presentation, which is a result of his reflection on Whitehead's statements that "speech is human itself,"[78] and that "expression is the one fundamental sacrament,"[79] is of crucial Christological importance. The various religions, including the Christian religion, are but re-presentations of a deeper faith that precedes them.

Logically, prior to every particular religious assertion is an original confidence and worth of life, through which not simply all our religious answers, but even our religious questions first become possible or have any sense. Hence the different historical religions, again including Christianity, can be thought of only as several attempts at a more or less self-conscious understanding of this original confidence. They are the results . . . of that original faith itself in search of a more fully conscious understanding of its own nature. . . . Because all religions are by their very nature representative, they never originate our faith, but rather provide us with particular symbolic forms through which that faith may be more or less adequately reaffirmed at the level of self-conscious belief.[80]

Religions are more or less valid inasmuch as they enable men and women to understand their confidence in the meaning of life.[81] Jesus as the Christ is normative for Christians because of his ability to re-present our ultimate significance.[82] "For the ground of faith and its object is not the Jesus who perfectly actualized the possibility of authentic faith and love, but the Jesus who decisively re-presents the possibility to us because, through the Christian witness of faith, he represents the primal word of God's grace, to which our own faith and love are always only the response."[83]

According to Ogden, to perceive the significance of Jesus Christ as the re-presentation of the truths of human existence is not to reduce Christ to be the exemplificator of timeless truths, but to insist on the responsibility of individuals to bring about the given possibility for human authenticity. Here the tension lies between affirming authentic existence as a factual possibility for all, mediated and communicated through any event, and its normative re-presentation in the Christ Jesus who is also historical. "The real meaning of the exclusiveness of Jesus Christ's lordship is not that divine lordship is exercised solely in that particular life, but rather that wherever such lordship is exercised and, that, naturally is everywhere, it can take no other form than the same promise and demand re-presented for us in Jesus."[84]

While for Ogden the ultimate meaning of Christology is strictly existential, yet the New Testament's insistence on the historicity of Jesus, its actual assertion about Jesus, seems to indicate that Christology cannot remain simply existential. Relative to this aspect, Ogden makes a distinction between the factual question about a fact—"What are the facts?"—and the metaphysical question—"What is it to be a fact?" While on the factual level one may be mistaken, this may not be so on the metaphysical level. Ogden relates that dichotomy to the historical level by making a distinction between empirical-historical and existential-historical. The existential is not essentially linked to the empirical. The fact "Jesus" is not taken with reference to the empirical-historical question: "What actually happened?" but to the existential-historical question: "What is the significance of what actually happened (or is taken to have happened) for human existence?" ". . . the Christian witness of faith takes certain things about Jesus to be empirically true in order to proclaim through them the very meaning of human existence."[85] What is important here is the assumption of fact, not the assertion of fact.[86] To affirm that Jesus is human is to be confronted in and through an historical existence with a demand to one's own existence.[87]

In Ogden's thought Jesus Christ cannot be viewed as the final or supreme and unique revelation of God. He rejects Bultmann's contention that authentic existence is only possible in Christ. For Ogden God's universal presence and revelation make authentic existence a universal possibility. "The decisiveness of Jesus Christ, the claim 'only in Jesus Christ,' is not that God is only to be found in Jesus and nowhere else, but that the only God who is to be found anywhere—though he is to be found everywhere—is the God who is made known in the word that Jesus speaks and is."[88] Since God's action in Jesus did not differ essentially from his action in other events, Jesus' Lordship, uniqueness, is primarily subjective. It is unique and decisive because someone perceives it as such. The specialness of God's action in Jesus Christ must be attributed to the beholder—the believer.

In refusing the classical doctrine of the incarnation Ogden has shifted the question about the finality and uniqueness of Christ from the objective to the subjective realm. This shift is evident in John Hick's position.

7. John Hick and the Myth of Incarnation

John Hick has outlined on several different occasions a position challenging traditional claims for the uniqueness of Christ.[89] He advocates a Copernican revolution in theology, a radical transformation in our conception of the universe of faith, "a shift from the dogma that Christianity is at the center, and that all the religions of mankind including our own serve and revolve around him."[90] Hick is advocating a shift from an ecclesiocentric to a theocentric understanding of the religions. In the context of this revolution, one cannot affirm Christianity to be true and all other religions false. This is ruled out by the Christian understanding of God whose love is universal in scope. "If God is the God of the whole world, we must presume that the whole religious life of mankind is part of a continuous and universal human relationship to him."[91] Hick is sharply aware of the theological implications of other religions. "Whereas it was hitherto reasonable to develop our theology in disregard to God's dealings with the non-Christian world, it has now ceased to be reasonable to do that."[92]

Religions, and this includes Christianity, are human cultural forms; it should not be assumed that their different apprehensions of God are mutually exclusive.[93] It becomes imperative for Christian theology to take stock of the fact that our literal interpretation of the incarnation has divisive and exclusivist consequences. The images through which the incarnation is expressed have no literal meaning; they are mythological.[94] Christianity's claim for the universality and uniqueness of Christ is based on the absoluteness of its experience. But this should not entail exclusiveness. Christ should be seen as mediating the presence and saving power of God in such a unique sense that no other religious figure has ever mediated it. The uniqueness of Christ has a purely devotional and subjective function. "That Jesus is my Lord and Savior is language like that of the lover, for whom his Helen is the sweetest girl in the world."[95] For a Christian, the claim to Christ's theological uniqueness is the product of a personal response to a way of life and salvation.[96] The Christian must not absolutize his point of view, assuming that it is a knowledge of things as they are in themselves, but it is a view of things as they are for him, things as they appear from his conditioned spatio-temporal standpoint. One community's affirmation does not contradict the affirmation of other communities, since each can be understood as expressing how God is related to them, and this involves only one aspect of God's nature.

Hick's position on the uniqueness of Christ has its correlates in his theology of the incarnation. In explaining the incarnation, he is unwilling to use substantive language. Instead he adopts dynamic categories of thought and derives his knowledge of God's nature from his knowledge of his deeds: "We know who and what he is insofar as we know what he has done."[97] Everything that Christianity knows concerning the divine attitude and activity toward mankind can be summarized in the assertion that God is *Agape.*

8. John A. T. Robinson: The Provisional Christ

God's nature is an operation, that of *agape,* which is revealed in the life and death of Jesus. In the life of Jesus, we find "not divine substance injected into a human frame, but divine action taking place in and through a human life."[98] Jesus' *agape* is not simply the representation of God's *agape;* it is the eternal divine *Agape* made flesh, inhistoricized, operating in a finite mode; but it is not identical with the whole of the infinite Agapeing.[99] The continuity between the divine Agapeing and the agapeing of Jesus is one of event rather than of entity, of activity rather than of substance. Christ is the Christian's image of God, and incarnation is an effective mythic expression of the Christian's appropriate attitude to God.[100] A similar approach is to be found in John A. T. Robinson's *The Human Face of God.*[101] While this book is not written specifically from the viewpoint of world religions, the author has spelled out in Chapter 7 his understanding of Christianity's claim for the uniqueness and finality of Christ. Robinson accuses Christian theologians of having turned the finality of Christ "into a static, finished, and, therefore, dead reality."[102] The author would rather speak of the "provisionality of Christ."[103] Christ is unique "not for anything exclusive to himself or finished in the past, but, in Teilhard's phrase, as the 'budding shoot' of the next development not only in man but in God."[104] The finality of Christ lies as much in the future as in the past. The Christian claims finality for Christ because he sees in Christ the all-embracing principle of interpretation of his experience. ". . . the Christian sees in Jesus the clue to (though not the exclusive embodiment of) the Christ, who in turn is the clue (though not the exclusive embodiment of) the nature of God as personal. . . ."[105]

Robinson's understanding of Christ's finality and uniqueness is underpinned by a specific understanding of the incarnation. He refuses to see the incarnation as an inbreaking of God into the human situation except in a symbolic sense. "The incarnation does not mean insertion into the living stream and intervention by God in the form of a man, but the embodiment, the realization of God in this man."[106] There is an explicit rejection of the doctrine of total immanence. The "realization of God" is a progressive one. "The Christ has been in the process—yes, in process—from the start, and in this sense we may speak of the 'eternal generation of the Son.' "[107] The Logos is "personalized" rather than hypostatized; God is made dependent upon man's response.[108]

In addressing the question whether Jesus is different from us in degree or in kind, Robinson states: "If one had to choose, I should side with those who opt for a degree-Christology."[109] For Robinson, Christ is unhinged from the historical Jesus, and can be found everywhere—in other religions.

9. Conclusion

This brief survey of Protestant positions underlines the fact that basic attitudes toward extra-Christian religions are linked to fundamental interpretation of the person of Jesus Christ. Avoidance or non-avoidance of the opposite poles of absolutism and relativism is dictated by Christology. Christologies that are incarnation-centered tend toward some form of exclusivity. Christianity in one form or another is seen as "the point of convergence" the "goal" or the "fulfillment" of other religions. Where the doctrine of the incarnation is challenged, there is evidence of a more relativistic approach. Christianity is seen as one form of religion having its own specific absoluteness. The question of absoluteness and uniqueness is a matter of subjective decision by individuals in specific traditions.

2
Roman Catholic Positions

1. Vatican II and Non-Christian Religions

In recent years, a number of Roman Catholic theologians have used Vatican II as a door through which to pass further elaboration of the Church's new respect for non-Christian faith and further exploration of the implications of that attitude.[110] Four basic documents from Vatican Council II deal with the various aspects of the question. The most important one is the *Declaration on the Relationship of the Church to Non-Christian Religions,*[111] and it is just that— a declaration. It provides no theological formulation for its position but simply a basic direction for the inter-religious dialogue. According to the Declaration, world religions are not simply "natural" realities but the bearer of God's word and presence.[112]

The material from these various documents, while rather restricted and meager both in scope and content, has created a renewed interest among Catholic theologians toward the non-Christian religions. The question about the nature of Jesus' uniqueness and function has been given new impetus.

These statements of Vatican II were prepared by earlier studies on membership in the Church, the salvation of the unbaptized, the universal salvific will of God, and the history of salvation and world history. The possibility of salvation for non-Christians has long been accepted by theology. The theologies of *votum fidei* or of the *desiderium sacramenti* are examples of the various ways on which such a possibility was founded. According to A. R. Schlette: ". . . it seems to be the case that non-Christians, whether envisaged as a category within sacred history or in regard to the possibility of their individual salvation, do not any longer present any very great difficulties for theology. . . . A real concrete chance of salvation exists for every individual, providing he lives according with his conscience."[113]

With Vatican II the question shifted from the possibility of salvation for non-Christians to the legitimate nature of extra-Christian religions as possible ways for God's presence and revelation. What is at stake today is the significance of religions as historical, social realities as they manifest and relate to the transcendent. Are extra-Christian religions possible ways of revelation and salvation? While there is a theology relative to the question of salvation for non-Christians there is very little theology concerning the legitimacy of extra-Christian religions as religions. In the classical Catholic system of dogmatic theology there is no clearly recognizable place in which the extra-Christian religions can be taken explicitly as a theme for discussion. The basic theological position underlying the Church's *Declaration on the Relationship of the Church to Non-Christian Religions* can be found in pre-conciliar theology which refers primarily to the *Logos spermatikos* of the Greek Fathers. The Declaration affirms of the Church: "Indeed, it proclaims and must ever proclaim Christ 'the way, the truth, and the life' (Jn. 14:6) in whom God has reconciled all things to himself."[114] Here the principle of Christianity's absoluteness is again affirmed; it is viewed as the plenitude and fulfillment of all other religions which are seen as stages, as "anticipatory phases" on the way to fulfillment.[115]

Contemporary Catholic theologians are attempting to come to terms with the theological fact of world religions. This attempt is taking place in light of two basic principles which have dominated the process in Catholic thought: the reality of God's universal salvific will and the claim that this will is revealed in a definitive way in the incarnation and by implication in the Church as the sacrament of that reality. These two principles have been affected by a radical shift which has occurred in the theology of revelation and redemption history, a change officially acknowledged in the *Constitution on Divine Revelation.*[116] In this understanding of revelation is the recognition of the redemptive involvement of God in the whole of human history. Here the universal salvific will of God becomes concretized historically as revelational and redemptive history.

2. Karl Rahner: The Christology of Quest

Karl Rahner is the Catholic theologian who has made the most important contribution in the application of the new theology of revelation and salvation history to the question of the intrinsic value of world religions. At the International Theological Conference held at Notre Dame in 1966, Rahner spelled out his understanding of the nature of the history of salvation and revelation.[117]

Rahner's position has its foundation in his understanding of revelation, grace, and anthropology and most basically in his Christology. In the past revelation has been understood primarily as a deposit of propositional truths given and transmitted by means of the Church. In this model of revelation all necessary truths were made known through Jesus Christ's preaching and handed down by the apostles and the Church. Accompanying this understanding, there is an on-going insistence that the explicitly Christian revelation is constitutive of salvation. Without the revelation in Christ, there is no salvific knowledge of God.

Rahner distinguishes between unthematic and thematic revelation, between transcendental and categorical revelation. Revelation is unthematic inasmuch as it is experienced not as an object within the world, but as the horizon within which the world is comprehended. Unthematic revelation is God speaking and communicating himself to mankind inwardly. This aspect of revelation is unthematic because it is known implicitly and existentially before it can possibly be understood explicitly and conceptually. God is present as revealer in the deep experiences of the believer and the beliving community. Transcendental revelation is co-existent and co-extensive with the history of the world and of the human spirit. It refers to God's gracious self-giving always and everywhere—to every person as the innermost center of his existence whether he wants it or not, whether he accepts it or not.

Historical revelation as expressed in Scripture and tradition is an event within the world that can serve to represent in an explicit way the truth of the graciousness of that horizon that is already known implicitly to encompass the world. There is therefore a universal history of salvation that co-exists with the history of mankind. Because of the universal divine presence human life can be lived in hope and trust. Life can be lived on the basis of a pre-conceptual "basic trust" in the value of existence.

God's Universal Salvific Will

Fundamental to Rahner's understanding of revelation is his understanding of the primacy of God's salvific will and the universality of grace. According to Rahner, God's will to save all beings is really God's will to bestow himself on the creature who is endowed with spiritual faculties. Salvation is not essentially a created gift, but God himself; it implies the self-bestowal of God and the possibility for the creature to receive what is offered. To be universal the reality of grace must be anticipated by the structure of man, by his openness and readiness to accept it.

The divine self-bestowal penetrates to the ultimate roots of a person, to the innermost depths, radically reorienting this person toward the immediate presence of God. It imparts to human nature an inward dynamism and an ultimate tendency toward God himself, a mode of being inserted into human nature which becomes an abiding element in its spiritual mode of being, as something that is a living force always and everywhere, whether accepted or rejected. It radically influences the ultimate development of a person's existence as spiritual. The transcendentality of a person as spiritual does not remain a separate department of human life over and above the historical context in which he is involved. The call to share supernaturally in God's life determines ontologically the nature of each human being.[118]

Inner and Outer Word

Categorical revelation can only be accepted and believed if it has some antecedent connection with the human mind. A message that is totally extrinsic to human life could not be accepted. The reason why men and women are able to believe the Gospel is that it corresponds to the redemptive reality which is already part of their lives. Rahner refers here to the inner word that addresses men and women in their history and summons them to faith. The outer word, categorical revelation, is credible because it corresponds to the inner word that God utters in the lives of all men and women.

The inner word, offered to all, never remains merely interior or individual, but it is exteriorized and takes social and historical forms; it takes the form of religions. There is a universal and on-going possibility for men and women to have a saving relation to God. And this saving relation can be found within the various and particular religions of various times and places. Non-Christians cannot be asked to achieve a saving relation to God outside the religion socially available to them.

As institutions, world religions can be seen as positive means of gaining the right relation to God, as means positively included in God's plan of salvation. We must rid ourselves of the prejudice that we can face world religions with the dilemma that it must either come from God in everything it contains and, thus, correspond to God's will and positive providence, or be simply a human construction.[119]

According to Rahner, Christianity does not simply confront the member of an extra-Christian religion as a mere non-Christian, but as someone who can and must already be regarded in this or that respect as an anonymous Christian.[120] Rahner interprets the non-Christian religions and the individual non-Christian as defined in a situation of anonymous or implicit Christianity. He does so while upholding the supernaturality of faith and the Christian character of salvation.

Anonymous Christianity

According to Rahner, ". . . the theory arose from two facts: first, the possibility of supernatural salvation and of a corresponding faith which must be granted to non-Christians even if they never became Christian; and, second, that salvation cannot be gained without reference to God and Christ, since it must in its origin, *history* and fulfillment be a theistic and Christian salvation. Anonymous Christianity has to do with the contrast between reflexive (or thematic) and unreflexive (unthematic) experience of God, a distinction that has to do with degrees of self-awareness."[121]

For Rahner the universal possibility of salvation does not reduce doctrinal and institutional forms to insignificance. While God's salvific grace is present in all human history, there is also a "history of salvation" where this saving grace is expressed in words and institutions. What anonymous Christianity means is that Christ and Christianity are, from one perspective, the manifestations of a possibility that is in principle present everywhere, and, from another perspective, the instruments through which that universal possibility can be manifested and known.

While Rahner's position on anonymous Christianity is rooted in his theology of revelation, the most fundamental objections made have been aimed at the Christology underlying it. Rahner has described this Christology as a "Christology of quest."[122] This Christology implies searching for something specific although yet unknown. Rahner affirms that a person who approaches human structures radically and without reserve "is always engaged upon a Christology of quest in his human existence."[123] While the seeker does not yet know that his goal is to be found in the person of Jesus Christ, yet he is prepared "to accept the goal wherever and however it can be found."[124]

The "Christology of quest" has its foundations in Rahner's Christology which is done within an anthropological horizon and in the framework of a "transcendental analysis." Rahner is interested in relating the context of the Christian faith to the fundamental meaning of human existence to correlate the essential structure of the human spirit with Christian faith, the mystery of God and the mystery of man.[125] Man is defined by Rahner as that which occurs when God gives of himself; man is the event of God's self-communication. Human nature should be conceived as an "active transcendence," as opening "toward the absolute being of God."[126]

The essence of man as obediential potency constitutes in its own way the transcendental presupposition for an incarnation:

> If human nature is conceived as an active transcendence toward the absolute being of God, a transcendence that is open and must be personally realized, then the incarnation

can be regarded as the (free, gratuitous, unique) supreme fulfillment of what is meant by "human being." Christ's *humanity* can be seen as that which results when God in his Word literally becomes other to himself in a creature. In this way, Jesus Christ is the summit of creation, the Lord and Head of the human race because he is one of its members, the "Mediator between God and creatures."[127]

Creation and incarnation are two adjacent acts of God, two moments in the process of God's self-communication. The incarnation is the definitive realization of the salvific presence of God at work throughout history.

Rahner's opponents have criticized this Christology because they see it as undermining and diminishing the qualitative uniqueness of the person and efficacy of Jesus Christ. While Rahner sees Jesus Christ as the examplar and fulfillment of any relationship with God, yet he is not to be seen simply as the one who has come to give a name to a reality which before him was nameless. Rahner does not simply see Jesus Christ as the manifestation of an "already given." Jesus Christ is an historical reality; he is unique precisely as the historical realization of human transcendence, as the occurrence of full divine offer and human acceptance which needs to happen only once for it to be a real possibility for all other persons.

As the unique occurrence of full divine offer and human acceptance, Jesus Christ has a universal causality. Rahner has attempted to answer one of the fundamental questions posed since Lessing relative to Christianity's claim about uniqueness and finality: What is the universal causality of the particular and historical event that Christ is? According to Rahner, it is not possible to look for an answer in the doctrine of the pre-existent Logos. Nor can the question be answered simply on the basis of the unity of mankind saved in its totality through the incarnation of the eternal Logos. According to Rahner: ". . . if the cross of Christ, his death and resurrection, are regarded as a saving event affecting all men, then even the notion of a universal communion of race and history shared by the Logos is not sufficient by itself. The death and resurrection of Jesus must possess universal importance in themselves for salvation and cannot merely be regarded as isolated events, of no significance in them-

selves in a life which only has universal relevance for salvation in being the life of the eternal Logos.[128]

Christ and Salvation

According to Rahner the salvific causality of the Christ event
should be understood as a "sacramental sign causality."[129] Christ is
perceived by Rahner as the primary sacrament "which is the original
sign and instrument of the innermost union with God and of the unity of the whole of mankind."[130] This sacramental causality is not the
cause of the universal salvific will, but is brought about by this universal salvific will. Yet God's universal salvific will and the Christ
event are not to be seen as two separate events set over against each
other simply as cause and effect. The sacramentality of the Christ
event belongs to the actualization of the divine salvific will which
finds in this sacramentality an irreversible historical expression.
Speaking about the incarnation Rahner writes: "This historically
tangible occurrence must be a *sign* of the salvation of the whole
world in the sense of a 'real symbol' and so possesses a type of causality where salvation is concerned."[131]

This kind of causality can only be fully understood if we place
it within the tasks Rahner assigns to his Christology which he sees
as transcendental. The purpose of transcendental Christology is to
remind us that the "idea of Christ" is necessary and that we have
the obligation of seeking for fulfillment in history, since we are not
that fulfillment and cannot be it. The primary aim of a transcendental Christology is to point out that the human person is Christ-ori-
ented and that in Christ he can find what he has always been seeking
for. The incarnation as event and symbol points to the basic truth
that man's transcendence is a transcendence of God.

Such a Christology does not lead to a transcendental deduction
of the Christ event from the human side; the human experience cannot simply deduce that God relates to human beings freely, either in
rejection or in acceptance. As symbol the Christ event not only leads
to an awareness of that what people are seeking, but also causes fulfillment historically, in its once-and-for-allness.

The consequences of Rahner's doctrine of the omnipresence of
grace is that Jesus is the complete and definite expression of a rela-

tionship between God and man already present potentially from the beginning and capable of being acknowledged at different times and different places. There is a single history of the dialogue between God and the world.[132]

Rahner's Christology is an attempt to affirm both exclusivism and universalism, to safeguard the uniqueness of Christ and also respect God's universal salvific will.[133] His doctrine of anonymous Christianity has been accused of elitism and of relativism.[134] In Rahner's mind, the anonymous Christian is not condemned to a defective form of Christianity; it exists at the same supernatural, radical and human level as that of the explicit Christian. The universal possibility of salvation is ontologically grounded in the creative act of God and made historically present in the Christ event. A possible misunderstanding of Rahner's position lies in the possibility of considering Christ as simply manifestation of that salvation and not as cause. In this case Jesus Christ would simply be objectifying and representing what was "always already" present to human reality, and the continuity between the particular and universal history of salvation is so emphasized that the uniqueness of the particular is threatened. These misunderstandings could be avoided if a greater historical dimension could be given to transcendental Christology and there were more emphasis on praxis.[135]

3. Raymond Panikkar: Universal Christology

Within the Roman Catholic context, one of the most influential attempts to relate theology positively to other religions has been Karl Rahner's theology of salvation history. This was accomplished by standing within the Catholic *Weltanschauung*. Rahner approaches extra-Christian religions primarily as a problem for theology.

Raymond Panikkar, another Roman Catholic theologian, is attempting to establish a positive encounter with extra-Christian religions by entering in the subjectivity of the other traditions. He is advocating an intra-religious dialogue as the model for the authentic interpretation of any contemporary religious experience. In his book The *Intra-Religious Dialogue* he affirms the following about his own personal journey: "I 'left' as a Christian, I 'found' myself a Hindu and I 'return' a Buddhist without ever having ceased to be a Christian."[136] Panikkar's approach is fundamentally ecumenical: extra-Christian religions are allowed to enter into the very center of religion and to permeate the structure of theology, Panikkar writes: "The real religious or theological task begins when the two views meet head-on beside oneself, when dialogue prompts genuine religious pondering and even a religious crisis at the bottom of man's heart: when inter-personal dialogue turns into intra-personal soliloquy."[137] The encounter of the world religions is constitutive of Christian theological reflection. In some way it is through the discovery of another religious tradition *ab intra* that Christianity rediscovers itself *ab intra*. The grounds of any authentic theology is a radical and fearless existential faith.

> The essence of faith seems to me to lie in the question rather than in the answer, in the inquisitive stance, in the desire rather than in the concrete response one gives. Faith is more the existential "container" than the intellectual content of "that thing" we try to describe. It belongs not only to those who respond correctly, but to all who authentically seek, desire, love, wish—to those of "good will."[138]

Panikkar has recently underlined an emerging tendency in the comparative study of religions: complementarity must be achieved within the individual himself.[139] "The burden of our tale is this: any inter-religious and inter-human dialogue, any exchange among cultures has to be preceded by an intra-religious and intra-human dialogue, an internal conversion within the person. We can only bridge the gulf between so many abysses, between East and West in this case, if we realize the synthesis and the harmony within that microcosm of ourselves."[140] Any encounter between religions demands this internal conversion, which Panikkar describes as a process of death and resurrection.[141]

The meeting of religions is a religious art, an art of incarnation and redemption. The laws of the inter-relation of cultures are not the same as those of the meeting between religions. A certain kenosis is needed for any fruitful encounter. "Christian faith must strip itself of the 'Christian religion' as it actually exists and free itself for a fecundation that will affect all religions both ancient and modern.

What we call Christianity is only one among other possible ones of living and realizing the Christian faith."[142] In his book *The Unknown Christ of Hinduism,* Panikkar suggested that the meeting of religions must be an existential one, that it must take place in Christ, in a Christ who does not belong to Christianity but to God.

In order to foster this necessary encounter, Panikkar calls for a "universal Christology." "Could we not develop an authentically universal Christology . . . a fundamental Christology which would make room not only for different theologies but also for different religions?"[143] This "universal Christology" is a form of Logos Christology developed by the early Fathers. There is a shift from the humanity of Christ to the Logos who by his relation to humanity is the center of the universe. Christ is the link between God and humanity.

> The reason to persist in calling it Christ is that it seems to be that, phenomenologically, Christ presents the fundamental characteristics of the mediator between divine and cosmic, eternal and temporal . . . which other religions call Isvara, Tathagata or even Jahweh, Allah and so on.[144]

The reality of Jesus as the Christ affirms his "hidden" presence in the religious history of mankind. It is the presence of Christ which opens the world religions and their individual adherents to the experience and reception of the "Christ event" and its efficacy. But this presence is manifold, as varied as the concrete forms of human religious history. Christ, then, is already the point of the encounter of Christianity and the world religions. In consequence, Christianity has a *sui generis* relationship, not an artificial one, with each of the world religions. Christ is the vital force of other religions.

> Christ is an ambiguous term. It can be the Greek translation of the Hebrew Messiah, or it may be the name given to Jesus of Nazareth. One may identify it with the Logos and thus with the Son or equate it with Jesus. The nomenclature that I personally would like to suggest in this connection is as follows: I would propose using the word Lord for that Principle, Being, Logos or Christ that other reli-

gious traditions call by a variety of names and to which
they attach a wide range of ideas.[145]

As the vital force of other traditions Christ is and must be more
than historical. "When I call this link between the finite and the infinite by the name Christ, I am not presupposing its identification
with Jesus of Nazareth."[146] "To say 'Jesus is the universal Savior'
means . . . that there is universal salvation, but that the Savior (the
Christ) is not an individual, not merely a historical figure nor basically an epistemological revealer."[147] Jesus is one of the names of the
cosmo-theandric principle, which has received practically as many
names as there are authentic forms of religiousness and which at the
same time finds an historically *sui generis* epiphany in Jesus of Nazareth.[148] What is important about Jesus the Christ is his personal dimension which can only be appropriated in love.[149]

The Christ of Faith

Since Christ is universal, he finalizes not just one but every great
religious tradition. He is the fulfillment of the aspiration of India as
much as Israel. It is unrealistic and unnecessary to require any tradition to renounce its heritage in order to accept Christ.[150] The finality and universality of Christ is not to be identified with the finality
or universality of the Christian religion. In fact, it would be nearer
the truth to say that Christ is the end of Christianity, as he is of Judaism. Panikkar approaches the distinctiveness of the Christian religion in a non-exclusive way with qualifiers which carry a "both-
and" rather than an "either-or" approach. While Christ is the
universal Savior, there are more saviors "embodying that saving
power which Christians believe to be the spirit of Jesus."[151]

For Panikkar the mystery of Christ extends far beyond any nar-
row particularity. But the question that needs to be asked in any encounter between Christianity and other religious traditions must be
the one of historicity and particularity. What can be said of the eternal Logos in light of the mystery of the incarnation must be said in
relation to Jesus of Nazareth, an individual human being who lived
in a specific place and time, who emerged out of a specific history
and gave impetus to a specific historical movement. While Panikkar

bly: Have not others realized the same thing for different groups of people? Are there not other incarnations, avatars? Would not the distinction between Jesus and others simply be one of degree and not of essence? The whole thrust of Küng's *On Being a Christian* is to prove that it is better to be a Christian than anything else. As sympathetic as Küng is to what is positive in great religious traditions, the main interest of his book is to emphasize what is unique and distinctive in the Christian message. In order to make an intelligent and responsible decision for Christianity one must claim such uniqueness for Christ and for Christianity. And what Küng perceives as distinctive in the Christian message is the person of Jesus Christ himself. The peculiarity, the singularity of Christianity is to consider Jesus Christ as definitive, decisive and normative for our relationship with God, with our neighbors and society.[164]

The Inductive Method

Küng judges other religions according to their concordance or non-concordance with Christianity. He seems to accept in an a priori way that Christ is the final norm for all religion and that other religions are ways of salvation "only in a relative sense, not simply as whole and in every sense."[165] He sees Christianity as a "cultural catalyst and crystallization point" for other religions."[166] While other religious traditions do have answers to our search for ultimate reality, their answers do not have the same value as that of Christianity. Christianity claims to have an adequate response to religious questions, and Küng maintains that this is a legitimate claim.

To establish this claim as legitimate, Küng employs the inductive method. It is his desire to lead his readers from a general openness to the ultimate human questions to an encounter with Christianity. Küng wants to avoid the extremes of dialectical theology, where the authority of God is overemphasized, and natural theology, where experience and reason are overemphasized.[167] Faith statements cannot simply be founded on biblical authority but must be verified from "the horizon of experience of man and society."[168] He writes in the same work: "The rules of the game in theological sciences are not in principle different from those of other sciences."[169] Experiencing reality and history is an important element of the theo-

accepts the incarnation of the Logos in Jesus and the necessity of history, he does insist that as Savior Jesus is the mythic and symbolic Christ at work in the universe of faiths. Panikkar's universal Christology, while original, seems to come out of a more traditional and "from above" approach. The importance here is focused on the eternal Logos and not on the historical Jesus. Panikkar affirms that Jesus Christ is not an historical person:

> We cannot limit Christ to an historical figure. To do this would imply denying his divinity. To begin with, Christ is not an historical *person;* his person is the divine person, who assumes in himself all history, but who is not "exhausted" in time. Christ really appears in history, and even becomes real flesh (John 1:14), and thus gets "entangled"—because of sin (2 Cor. 5:21)—in the temporal rhythm of the cosmos, in order to "disentangle" it from mere temporality, but he cannot be identified with a simple *avatara,* with a mere "incarnation" of the divine, i.e., a descent of God at a given moment for a particular or universal purpose. The Christian conception of the incarnation is essentially linked with the Trinity. Were the Absolute not Trinity, then Christ could only be an *avatara,* but not the *alpha* and *omega,* the beginning and the end, the only mediator, he through and for whom all has been made and in whom all things subsist.[152]

We have here a very classical approach to Christology, with all the difficulties that have emerged from this approach.

4. Hans Küng: The Historical Jesus

With Hans Küng we have another positive approach to the world religions but with different reasons, a different methodology and Christology. In Küng's position is apparent the effect of two elements operative in the Protestant positions: an understanding of the incarnation as mythical and the use of an inductive method in association with the historical-critical method.

Küng's position on world religions is amply expressed in his book *On Being a Christian*. Earlier in 1964, in a paper prepared for the 38th International Eucharistic Congress in Bombay, he stressed the need for a more positive attitude on the part of Christians toward other religions. He then felt that it was impossible for Christianity to exist in isolation from other religions. The great religions of the world all give testimony to the fact that there is a God. These religions are in a position to respond to questions which are raised concerning God.

This position raises basic Christological questions. Küng approaches Christology inductively from below and insists on the necessity of the historical-critical method to discern the essence of Jesus' message and the import it had on his followers. "It is better ... not to postulate and deduce theologically from above divine sonship, pre-existence, creation, incarnation, but, as we are attempting to proceed, by way of induction and interpretation from below."[153]

Küng claims throughout the book that we can know historically Jesus' way of life, even his self-awareness: "We know incomparably more that is historically certain about Jesus of Nazareth than we do about the great founders of the Asian religions."[154] On the basis of historical knowledge of the life of Jesus he bases his claim that Jesus is superior to all other founders of great religions.

The use of the historical and critical inductive method and the individual method leads Küng to a particular understanding of the person of Jesus Christ. In his Christology he does not proceed from the presupposition of the reality of God and the incarnation of the Logos, but from the history of Jesus in order to find out how this leads to the recognition of his divinity.

Incarnation and the Historical Jesus

According to Küng, the incarnation as a way of understanding the mystery of Christ detracts from the essential aspect of the Christian message.[155] The incarnational approach leads to a simplistic identification of Jesus to God[156] and stresses an ontological approach to Jesus Christ.

Küng sees the shift that took place during the early phases of the Church's history, from Christology centered on the cross and resurrection to one centered on the incarnation, in a negative way,

as a process of Hellenization. The process is exemplified in v place relative to the term "Son of God." Küng affirms that originally pointed to "the legal and authoritative status Christ in the Old Testament." Through the process of He the same title points to "his descent. . . . It is a question le tion than of essence."[157]

A literal understanding of the incarnation is not p Küng. He sees the incarnation as a mythical expression "that the relation between God and Jesus did not emerge later stage and as it were by chance but existed from th and had its foundations in God himself."[158] Küng conte idea of incarnation was one of the many mythical p which the first Christians tried to articulate the meanir for them.

The task of Christology today is not that of repeati tologies of the past, either of the New Testament or of it is to create a new translation that would be "oriente nal text and learn from the mistakes and strong poi translations."[159] Chalcedon needs to be retranslated in way: "The true man Jesus of Nazareth is for faith the of the one true God."[160] In his life, being and action, Je "God's word and will in human form."[161]

Küng has his own understanding of the incarna tional and not essential; it underlines what Jesus h manity. Jesus is understood as being the advocate, th of God to us. "God himself as man's friend was p speaking, acting and definitely revealing himself in establishes his own list of titles for Jesus: God's " uty," "delegate," "spokesman," "plenipotentiary." not to be understood in a legalistic fashion. Jesus i a deeply intimate, existential sense, a personal am confidant, friend of God."[163]

By challenging the traditional doctrine of the is at the same time challenging the traditional f Church's claim to the uniqueness of Christ. If th not imply a pre-existent Logos entering human h all in order to transform and change it, but is sir of Jesus as "God's representative," then the que

logical science. "The experience of reality accessible to every man will be inductively elucidated, in order . . . to place him before a rationally responsible decision which claims more than merely pure reason—which claims in fact the whole man."[170]

Küng cannot establish his claim for Jesus' uniqueness on the incarnation. He offers a variety of reasons why Jesus and his message surpass all others.[171] These reasons are arrived at inductively. Yet the historical and inductive methods cannot establish the normativeness of Jesus Christ; they cannot establish why it is Jesus who becomes God's representative rather than another. It is on the basis of an historical knowledge of Jesus' life that Küng establishes his claims that Jesus was like no other man, that he is the norm for all others. Yet many scholars have cautioned about appealing to the way Jesus lived in order to conclude about his being the ultimate norm for all other religious figures.[172]

Küng rejects the notion of the "anonymous Christian"[173] as an offensive term for non-Christians. Yet the problem that this concept attempts to meet is a very real one. While Jesus remains the universal norm and other religious traditions retain their own value, how is Jesus Christ related to these religions?

While Küng admits that Jesus Christ is the universal Savior[174] and that non-Christians can be saved,[175] he does not relate the non-Christians to Jesus Christ in a causal way. His understanding of resurrection leaves no room for a causal relation other than a remembering and a recollecting of his words and deeds by explicit Christians. For those who have not been in contact with the message of Jesus Christ, such a relationship to Christ is impossible. There is no causal link between Jesus Christ and the salvation of men other than a gnoseological one.

Küng's position does not seem ultimately to differ from the fulfillment theory. What is positive in other religious traditions can be brought to full realization in Christianity.[176] In fact the Christian proclamation is needed in order "that God may not remain to them (the non-Christians) the unknown God."[177] For Küng the world religions as ways of salvation play an inferior role. The non-Christian has the right and duty to seek God in his own religion until such time as he is confronted in an existential way with the revelation of Jesus Christ.

3
Inclusive and Exclusive Christologies

1. Exclusive Christology

The Christologies previously discussed took their problematic from the kinds of questions raised by the on-going encounter of Christianity with world religions. Their formal context is the basic question of the nature of the assertion made about the unique salvific mediatorship of Jesus, when such a claim is made over against the contemporary assertions of other religious traditions. Our survey of various Christologies has unearthed a wide range of substantive differences. In an attempt to sort out these differences and to shed light on the problematics that still need to be dealt with, I will now set forth a variety of classifications of Christologies.[178] The classifications vary according to the focusing element employed. The first classification focuses on the basic openness of various Christologies to extra-Christian religions as possible ways of salvation. There are two basic forms of Christology: an exclusivist and an inclusivist Christology. An exclusivist Christology implies that salvation can only be found in and through Jesus Christ. According to this view there is no truth, no genuine relation to God to be found outside of the Christian faith. This view is represented by Karl Barth and his disciples. Barth based his approach on a very sharp distinction between religion and revelation. Religion is seen as negative, as a human attempt to reach God, while revelation is God's outreach to man and woman. This outreach takes place uniquely in Jesus Christ. Barth emphasizes the absolute transcendence of God in relation to man and stresses the opposition between biblical eschatology and an immanent world eschatology, between salvation history and world history. Revelation in Jesus Christ is characterized by its utter gratuitousness; it is a summoning to decision and a call for a confession of faith.

2. Inclusive Christology

Contemporary theologians, both Catholics and Protestants, do not follow Karl Barth in this form of exclusivism. Their Christologies are better described as inclusive. This type of Christology sees Jesus Christ as the fulfillment of human history, the liberator, the embodiment of our highest aspirations, and the perfect unsurpassable expression of what it means to be human, of authentic humanity. An inclusivist Christology, while placing Jesus Christ at the very center of Christian self-understanding and human self-understanding, views Jesus Christ as disclosive in an explicit way of God who is present to all human reality implicitly and always. In this Christology Jesus is already the revealer of a decisive truth about God and human existence; yet this is not necessarily true for individuals of other traditions. This Christology excludes the possibility of other revelation being equal to that of Christ and insists that all other religions and religious figures need to be judged and completed by Christ. Christianity is seen here as the summit and completion of all other religions; it is the fulfillment of what is best and true in the others. This position is clearly stated by E. O. James. He writes about Christianity: "In it the highest insights of Judaism, Islam, Zorastrianism, Hinduism and Buddhism have been realized, fulfilling alike the prophetic revelation and mystical knowledge of God and of sacramental union with him in its transcendental and immanental aspects."[179]

This is the most predominant stance among Protestant and Catholic theologians, although at times quite hidden. While extra-Christian religions can, though incomplete and imperfect, be caught up in a positive salvation and revelation history, they do need to con-

quer their ambivalence and finally accept Jesus Christ, the eschatological Word of God. What is positive in other religious traditions
can be brought to full realization only in Christ. While having de-
parted from an exclusivist Christology, contemporary theologians
still make a very sharp judgment on the difference of quality between
Christian revelation and all other revelation.

While it is acknowledged by these theologians that divine revelation takes place in the lives of all men and women, the implicit,
hidden and conditioned presence of the divine to human life is fully
spelled out, openly proclaimed and irrevocably concretized in the
person of Jesus Christ and his message.

3. Logos Christology

The oldest and constantly renewed Christology underlying this
inclusivistic approach is the Logos Christology founded on the universal presence of the Logos.[180] This view was already present in the
Logos Christology of the second-century apologists. They found *Lo-
goi spermatikoi,* fragments of the one Logos, at work everywhere in
the world. The Logos is the cosmic principle of order, the ground of
meaning, and the source of purpose. The Logos, in its transcendence,
is timeless and infinite; its historical effects are dynamic and ever
changing. According to J. Cobb, "the Logos is immanent in all
things as the initial phase of their subjective aim, that is, as their fundamental impulse toward actualization."[181] Logos Christology claims
that the divine Logos is present in all things and that it is incarnate
in Jesus of Nazareth.

This Christology has taken these different directions in contemporary theology depending on the basic framework employed. One
of these approaches uses an evolutionary framework and is found
primarily in Teilhard de Chardin's interpretation. Teilhard sees the
presence of the Logos as the matrix of potentialities that make up an
evolving world. The Logos must permeate all things, and evolution
must be seen as fully realized in the person of Jesus Christ. The incarnation is seen as an act co-extensive with the duration of the
world. The second approach is not cosmological but anthropological.
The Logos is present to all human reality as possibility for a self-
communication of God. The incarnation is seen here as the unique

and highest instance of the essential completion of human reality and Christology is the absolute expression of anthropology. This approach is represented by Karl Rahner and his concept of anonymous Christianity.

4. Logos and History

The third approach is historical. The Logos is understood primarily as opening the dimension of history to ultimate fulfillment. Here the question of the meaning and salvation of the individual person becomes the question of the meaning and salvation of history as a whole. God's revelation and man's salvation are accomplished in normal human history. For Pannenberg there is one history: history is salvation history. The meaning of each historical event, and this includes the Christ event, becomes definitive and only fully evident in the context of the universal, final meaning of history as a whole. This approach has been taken up primarily by Pannenberg. He interprets Jesus Christ as the proleptic presence of the ultimate end of history. These various approaches express an inclusivistic Christology. They admit that God and his salvation are present also in extra-Christian religions. They do pose the basic question about the continuity between Christ and these extra-Christian religions, the question about the causal relationship between the Christ-event and the salvation that occurs in these various religious ways. As Logos-Christologies they reflect in a very special way the tension that exists between the universalistic tendency of the eternal Logos and the particularistic tendencies of the historical Jesus within Christology. They pose the question of the relation of the Christ of faith and the Jesus of history.

There is an on-going danger to all Logos Christology of denying value to the concrete and the historical humanity of Christ. The manifestation of the Logos in the concrete historical individual of Nazareth has no uniqueness of its own. The basic thrust of a Logos Christology is that the logical subject of Christological affirmation is not the historical Jesus of Nazareth but the eternal Logos. Christological affirmations have a logic of their own; they are connected to Jesus of Nazareth through some mediating faction, be it the cosmos, human reality or universal history.[182]

5. Soteriology

In order to understand the subtleties of the various Christologies as they attempt to deal with the fact and presence of salvation in extra-Christian religions, another classification is needed. The form of this classification is the place, necessity and causal relationship attributed to Jesus relative to the salvation of mankind. What is it that binds us to Jesus Christ? How can the incarnation, the cross and the resurrection of the Lord be made to relate in a real sense to the salvation of all? What does the unique historical action performed by Jesus Christ have to do with the salvation of men and women of different generations and times? What is the nature of Jesus' mediation that makes it in a sense more final and absolute than that of others? The nature of Christ's causal relationship to universal salvation is anchored in the very nature of his person so that this classification, like the previous one, has its foundation in the fundamental question of the nature of Christ.

6. George Rupp: Christologies and Cultures

In relation to the causal relation of Jesus Christ to the salvation of mankind several possible classifications can be arrived at. One of these classifications is found in G. Rupp's book *Christologies and Cultures.*[183] Rupp's basic contention is that past attempts at explaining the nature of Christ's redemptive work demonstrate different world views. The author argues for the possibility of relating systematically the various Christological controversies to opposite world views. Rupp sees clear implications between various Christological types and different ways of interpreting "the fact of religious pluralism."[184] Interpretations of religious pluralism can be differentiated in reference to variables in Christology.[185] These variables concern primarily the significance attributed to the redemptive work of Jesus Christ. "To take the point at which the connection is most direct, the way in which a given interpreter of the atonement treats the ephapax—the once-and-for-all claim for the work of Christ—cannot but have implications for his approach to non-Christian religious tradition."[186]

Rupp has chosen here to deal primarily with soteriology, affirming that doctrinal definitions concerning the person of Jesus are directly related to the perception of the nature of his work.[187] He sees two major focuses to post-medieval interpretations of the significance and consequence of Christ's redemptive action: as a transaction of universal implication, or as the significance of an historical event.[188] While the author sees these two alternatives as deficient and polarizing, his typology is grounded in these two positions. It employs two sets of variables: the realist vs. the nominalist, and the traditional vs. the processive.[189]

According to Rupp, the realist perceives Christ as having assumed a universal human nature and his redemptive work as having altered the general and universal situation of mankind. The nominalist focuses on the influence of the historical Jesus on the individual believer. The significance of Christ is seen here as inseparable from the influence of his teachings. The emphasis is on a universally valid truth and on Christ as teacher and as example.

The transactional and processive variables are not directly concerned with the value of the work of Christ, but with the manner in which this redemptive work affects individuals and the world. While a transactional model sees the effect of Christ's atonement as transcending the normal, historical process, and as a-temporal and independent of historical mediation, the processive model respects the norms of spatial-temporal existence. Both sets of variables are therefore concerned with the classic question of subjective and objective redemption—a question that has deep epistemological ramifications.

It is Rupp's contention that religious pluralism is inadequately interpreted if based on a realist-transactional or nominalist-transactional Christology. The author advocates a processive approach that allows an appropriation of the realist and nominalist commitments and respects the historical context and the concrete data of all religious traditions, including the Christian.[190] A processive view considers the entire action of atonement as taking place in time and "emphasizes the fact of development and a belief in increase in being and/or value in individual selves, in the cosmic process, or even in God."[191] The processive model respects the social and cultural forms of mediation of Christ's influence.[192]

The change which Christ's work effects is not in principle complete apart from the temporal appropriation of this work, and the realization of salvation cannot abstract from historical development. The processive position attempts to do justice to the thoroughly historical character of human existence. It attends specifically to the questions of the historical mediation of Christian teaching.

While in the realist-transactional approach no one attains salvation apart from Christ, a position which results in an ecclesiastical exclusivism, a processive view can entertain the possibility of salvation apart from Jesus Christ.

7. Peter Schineller: Christ's Causality

Another classification with the same basic focus has been developed by Peter Schineller.[193] He sees three basic categories that apply to Jesus Christ's causal relationship to salvation; it is either constitutive and normative, normative but not constitutive, or neither normative nor constitutive.

Perceived as constitutive, Jesus Christ's mediation is essential to salvation; Jesus' mediation is the efficient cause of the saving grace in the world. Without the historical incarnation, no person would be saved. Jesus Christ is the condition apart from which there cannot be authentic existence and salvation. There can be no revelation outside the physical reality of Christ, nor can there be any justification. A constitutive understanding of Christ's mediation can lead to either an exclusivist or an inclusivist Christology. As an inclusivist Christology, this particular approach will attempt to discern how and in what ways those who have no explicit knowledge of Christ are affected by Christ's causality. Rahner's "anonymous" Christology is such an approach.

In the second classification the key word is "normative." Normative indicates a measure, a superior or ideal type, that can function to correct and judge all others. As normative Jesus Christ's salvific mediation corrects and fulfills whatever other mediations of salvation have occurred either in the past, present or future. While "Jesus Christ is the normative way to God and his salvation . . . he is neither the exclusive nor the constitutive way. Salvation, which was always possible for all mankind, becomes decisively and normatively manifest in Jesus."[194]

While the first category, Jesus Christ as the constitutive of salvation, can be arrived at only through a decision of faith, the second position can be a deduction from the New Testament seen as authoritative source or from a comparison of Christianity with other traditions. Küng's position is arrived at in both ways.[195] In this category the absence of the Christ event would not result in the absence of salvation but of a decisive manifestation and ephiphany of salvation.[196] There is no intrinsic connection between creation and incarnation, as in Rahner's position.

8. Christology and Pluralism

The last category is one in which Jesus Christ's mediation is seen neither as constitutive nor as normative in relation to salvation. In this position there are many mediators of salvation, and Jesus Christ is one of them. It is impossible with the limited amount of knowledge that we have, and in light of the incomprehensibility of God as ultimate mystery, to conclude about the uniqueness and normativeness of Jesus Christ as mediator. This is a position of relativism. Each religion expresses the religiosity of a particular culture. This position seems to be reflected in John Hick, Don Cupitt and others.

While Jesus is perceived as a mediator and catalyst for religious values, he is not to be universalized. Jesus is the historical mediator of a unique experience which need not be accepted as a universal mediation. What has been mediated is not irreducibly bound up with the person of Jesus. According to P. Tillich it is the biblical picture of Jesus that has transforming power, not the hypothetical man behind the picture. Yet because the religious values associated with Jesus have historical importance, believers inspired by him will be constantly creating new images of Jesus out of earlier material. The significance of Jesus lies precisely in the relevance of his image for understanding that final and universal reality which confronts men and women in various events. Here there is no need to conclude that the irreducibility of Jesus Christ consists in the fact that he is the sole agent of God. There is place for the "sentness" of other religious leaders past and still to follow. Neither the Jesus of history nor the Christ of faith is a closed personality.

9. Don Cupitt

It is difficult to reconcile this last position with the traditional affirmations made about the uniqueness and once-and-for-all nature of Jesus' mediation and with the traditional understanding of the incarnation. Those who advocate this position have also challenged the classical doctrine of the incarnation. The classical foundation for the finality and uniqueness of Christ is faith's perception of Christ's unique relation to God, the perception that there is a unique embodiment of God in Christ. Jesus as the mediation of pre-existing divine Wisdom or Logos is understood as absolutely unique among all humans. If the incarnation is not taken literally, then one of the basic foundations for Christ's uniqueness is removed. Don Cupitt formulates well the difficulties that many theologians have with the *classical* doctrine of the incarnation. "The eternal God and an historical man are two beings of quite different ontological status. It is simply unintelligible to declare them identical."[197] In the Gospels, Christ does not appear as one who embodies God, "but as one who with the whole of his passionate nature witnesses to God."[198] According to the author, "it was always a mistake to make Jesus himself the direct object of worship."[199] His mission was not to draw attention to himself, but to be a signpost, to point to God. "Jesus' legacy to mankind is an urgent appeal to each of us to acknowledge above all else the reality of God."[200]

To obviate the danger of absolutizing Christianity's claim to Christ's uniqueness, Cupitt prefers a Christology of Jesus as the Word of God instead of Jesus as God's Son. According to Cupitt, we should not think of Christ as Son or image, but as Word and Witness. Jesus' finality does not lie in himself but in what he proclaims, and in the way he bears witness to it. "He is final because of the way he bears witness to what is final and unsurpassable."[201] By separating Jesus' uniqueness from his person and relating it to his witnessing, Cupitt attempts to avoid pure religious relativism and the absolutist language in which traditional Christian faith has so often been expressed.

Yet if the incarnation is no longer accepted as a one-time descent of God to earth, if it is meant to express Jesus' representation of God's love, then the following question is unavoidable: Have not others carried out essentially the same role? Can we not speak of other incarnations? As Cupitt writes:

> God can be believed in and served in as many ways as there are people. In the Christian tradition, Jesus is the paradigm of faith, but that paradigm may be re-enacted in a great variety of ways, and we need not labor to reduce their number.[202]

Where the doctrine of the incarnation is challenged, there is evidence of a more relativistic approach to Christ's uniqueness and finality. Is it possible to say that the Logos was incarnate in Gautama and in that incarnation realized certain perfections unrealized in Jesus? That seems a drastic move insofar as it abandons the historical claim of one unique incarnation. The basic distinction made between "inclusive" and "exclusive" Christologies does not seem adequate. While the positions are described as "inductive" yet allow for and include the positive and salvific content of other religions, they insist that these religions are simply preparations for Christianity. Christianity alone has received the final revelation. Other religions remain only as temporary ways. No matter how complicated the arguments are in the inclusivist positions, it is still a question of superior/inferior. Within the history of religious consciousness the Christian religion has always assumed the role of transforming the other religious traditions.

A Dialogical Approach

What is needed is a dialogical approach toward extra-Christian traditions which, while accepting the universal meaning of Jesus, does not approach other religions with a priori claims of exclusivist normality. J. Moltmann's point is well taken here: ". . . they (the non-dialogical positions) are still not based on dialogue since they proceed from the Christian monologue, not from the dialogue itself. They all formulate the Christian position before they enter into dialogue. They do not formulate it in the context of dialogue."[203] On the same point J. Macquarrie writes: "A creative dialogue is possible only if there is complete openness, and no preliminary assumption that one revelation must be the yardstick for all others."[204]

In the search for a truly non-exclusivist Christology one essential question needs to be asked: What are the parameters for Christology?

There are some ways of interpreting Christology that destroy the possibility of dialogue with other faiths and make a non-exclusivist Christology impossible. There are problems in the understanding of incarnation that must be cleared up before genuine Christian openness can be carried through.

The contemporary Christologies that have taken seriously the challenge of world religions have made clear the difficulties underlying the construction of a non-exclusivist Christology. These Christologies incorporate one or more elements and difficulties resulting from the development of modern Christology.[205] This development began with the humanistic thrust of Schleiermacher's Christology. Christology is held in the closest relation to anthropology. The second important moment is the Christology developed by Hegel. The importance here is the global approach taken to Christology and the importance given to the Trinitarian pattern. The Trinity can be seen as an archetype of unity and diversity drawing together world religions.

A third important moment in the development of Christology is Bultmann's existential approach. The decisive question according to Bultmann's existential Christology is whether Christ helps me because he is God's Son, or whether he is Son of God because he helps me. Christology is subsequent to soteriology. A Christological pronouncement is not primarily a description of Jesus Christ, but a confession of his meaning for the follower.

Contemporary Christologies, emerging in the consciousness of other religious traditions, are characterized by their concern for the correlation of Christology to anthropology, for the universal dimension of Christ as Logos and for the existential meaningfulness of

Christ for every contemporary Christian. These characteristics focus sharply on the basic problem of contemporary Christology—the relationship of the historical Jesus to the Christ of faith, or of the universalization of religious meaning, and the radicalization of the special occasion itself.[206] They bring to the fore the basic question being asked about Christianity's relation to other religious traditions: Does the grounding of the universal possibility of salvation derive from the historical work of Jesus or from the divine intention as is expressed in the on-going process of creation?

All three elements have been objected to since, in different ways, they appear to trivialize the historical dimension of the Christ event. Self-transcending anthropology is seen as inadequate because it leaves out the indispensable element of history. Christology cannot be reduced simply to an extension of anthropology. An anthropological approach leads to a priorism where Jesus becomes the occasion of faith, not the object or the cause of faith. The call to faith does not come from history, but from an a priori existential. The revelation in the Jesus event is verified on the basis of its ability to meet the requirements of a person's pre-understanding of himself. Jesus as the Christ event is true because he fulfills human needs.[207] This anthropological approach to Christology gives rise to different theories of "anonymous Christianity."[208] Some see in this concept the danger of seeing Jesus Christ simply as coming in order to give a name to a reality which existed before him as nameless. They see the danger of explaining Christ in light of the religions instead of the religions in the light of Christ. The tendency is to interpret the incarnation as the historization of an archetype that is already found throughout the history of religions.[209]

The renewal of Logos Christianity, while deeply rooted in tradition, has been strongly influenced by Hegel's theology. In Hegel's thought, it is through the Son that the Father enters the world and the world is led back to the Father in the Spirit. While Hegel sees the eternal as prior to the temporal, he does not devalue history since the Spirit can only be actualized in the movement of history. Yet many Hegelians have played down the value of the historical and the particular in their own Christologies. Certain forms of Hegelianism lead to the swallowing up of history in timeless truths, of the particular and concrete in the universal and abstract.

The existential dimension of contemporary Christology has insisted on the "for us" aspect of God and Christ. This has been objected to as a dehistorization of the kerygma, the breaking of the continuity of history into existential moments, the dissolution of the history of salvation into the historicity of existence.[210] Jesus is made Christ through a value judgment.

The objections to all three dimensions of contemporary Christology may be reduced to the following: they reduce Christ to a symbol of some timeless truths and, therefore, trivialize this historicity and his uniqueness. Jesus and the event of salvation history become mere symbols of a wider universal truth about God rather than a once-and-for-all unique manifestation of God otherwise unknowable.

Conclusion

One of the basic tensions encountered in the contemporary Christologies previously described lies between claims for the universal and active presence of Christ and the particularity of Jesus, the one who died on the cross. The Christological problem can be expressed in terms of the Jesus of history and the Christ of faith.[211] In fact it has been claimed that the historical particularity of Jesus, Lord and Christ, is the source of Christian exclusivism. At the same time that this is affirmed, there has been since the Enlightenment the admission that the affirmation of a universal significance for Jesus of Nazareth must be understood as a pre-critical judgment. No historical person or event can be given an absolute status; historical statements are always open and reversible. An historical person and some historical events can express absolute values, yet no essential links can exist between the two. What is being denied through this understanding of history is what appears to be the very heart of the Christian message: the basic link between the person of Jesus and God's salvific will. It is claimed that the very heart of the Christian faith consists of an affirmation in faith of God's saving action in history and that decisivity in the life of Jesus of Nazareth.

1. The Historical Jesus

Notwithstanding these affirmations, it appears that the only way to deal with Christianity's claim for Jesus Christ in a non-exclusivistic way is by emphasizing the historical dimension of the Christ event. Only when the Christian distinctiveness and identity are to some extent historically localized will it be possible to pose the question about the relationship of Christianity to other religions in an authentic dialogical way. Claims to absoluteness and uniqueness have to be dealt with historically, in the concrete, social and historical dimension of reality. The Christian truth about human reality must necessarily be deciphered at the very heart of a contingent history, that of Jesus Christ. Human history, in all its contingency and particularity, cannot be adventitious to Christian faith. History cannot be bypassed. There is no immediacy to God, not even in the Christ event. Existential interpretations tend to a simultaneity with Christ that would collapse the past and future into a present of personal decision.

Historical in all of its dimensions, the Christ event has been made known from generation to generation historically, through the Scriptures. Here the past, however distant and disturbing, cannot be neutralized or objectified by its contemporary interpreter. Texts must be read, responded to amid a welter of conflicting interpretations. The diversity of traditions cannot be reduced to a comforting constant, itself immune to historical change or independent of personal commitment. The irreducible diversity of Christian tradition must be respected. Contrary to all idealist hermeneutics, the Scriptures exist only in specific, finite, historically conditioned expressions. Whatever authority may be given to the Scriptures, this authority is marked by the historical nature of Scripture.

2. A Christology from Below

A dialogical and non-exclusivistic Christology must take into consideration the radical historicity of its founding event, the Christ event, and of its source, the Scriptures. As such it will necessarily be a Christology whose point of departure is from below. A Christology "from above" is one that directs itself first of all to the divinity of Jesus. W. Pannenberg writes: "For Christology that begins 'from above,' from the divinity of Jesus, the concept of the Incarnation stands in the center."[212] In a Christology "from above" the doctrine of the Trinity is presupposed and the question asked is: How has the Second Person of the Trinity (the Logos) assumed a human nature? K. Rahner described the Christology "from above" as "the metaphysical type."[213] In this Christology "the pre-existence of the Logos," his divinity, his distinction from the Father, and the predicate "Son of God" ascribed to the divine Logos as he who pre-exists in this Christology are regarded as manifestly belonging to him from the first, and assumed more or less to be statements based upon the verbal assertions and convictions of Jesus himself.[214]

Macquarrie suggests what seems to be a very important step for any contemporary Christology: the incarnational framework "must emerge only at the end and not be presupposed."[215] Pannenberg has already made the point. "Methodological reasons," he affirms, "do not permit us to work with the incarnation as a theological presupposition. To do so would be to make the humanity of Jesus' life problematic from the very beginning. To be sure, all Christological considerations tend toward the idea of the incarnation; it can, however, only constitute the end of Christology. If it is put instead at the beginning, all Christological concepts are given a mythological tone."[216]

What is being asked by Macquarrie and Pannenberg is a methodological shift, a Christology whose starting point is "from below." A Christology "from below" directs itself to the historical man, Jesus. According to Rahner, the starting point for a Christology from below "is the simple experience of the man Jesus, and of the resurrection in which his fate was brought to its conclusion."[217] "Jesus in his human lot is *the* (not a!) address to God and man, and as such eschatologically unsurpassable."[218] A Christology "from below" views the life, ministry, passion and death and resurrection of Jesus as an act of God's self-giving. The title of Jesus is the revelation of God's self-giving love. A Christology from below simply states that all Christological language must take its beginning in the historical Jesus; and this historical man, Jesus, is the criterion of Christology. The historical Jesus is the locus where one can learn to speak about God. Starting "from below" is not an attempt to prove the divinity of Jesus from his own history. In Jesus there is movement from above—from God to Jesus where Jesus is the receiver. The resurrection is the expression of this movement.

What characterizes an approach from below is its openness. As Schillebeeckx writes:

> But then the best way into the distinctive nature of Jesus of Nazareth, in his significance for all, it seems to me, is indeed not to approach him either from a given idea of what "being God" means or from a preconception of what "being man"—and thus being-a-human-person—really entails. It will not do to fit together two models or two concepts—"being man" and "being God"—so as to arrive in that way at a conceivable (or inconceivable) "amalgam" of a "Godman," for which Jesus of Nazareth might then have been an historical occasion. Going to Jesus in order to find in him salvation is to approach him in a state of ignorance, or, better, of "open knowledge," of what "being man" properly means, and likewise what "being God" means, perhaps in order to learn from him the real content of both—and *that* precisely through their interrelation as manifested in Jesus. Of course we have definite conceptions of man as also of God, just as the Jews had when they encountered Jesus. Jesus himself stood within the tradition of the peculiar Yahwistic Jewish experience of God. This already given understanding is in no sense disavowed. But we are asked to be open to Jesus' own interpretative experience of the God-reality which he manifests in his "being man."[219]

Christianity proclaims that Jesus as the Christ reveals the true force of God and the true force of man, the true force of God being revealed in the true force of man. What this implies is that we have to speak about Jesus Christ in historical tones as well as in faith language, that we have to distinguish between Jesus' historical significance for us and his unique universal significance. How these two total aspects are to be understood is the fundamental Christological problem.

3. The Humanity of Jesus

In the context of a Christology from below, the unique universality of Jesus' significance for us must be perceived within the dimensions of Jesus' humanity. As Schillebeeckx writes: "If Jesus of Nazareth is declared to be the eschatological definitive, saving action of God, this must be something available to religious experience and discussion in faith-language with as its starting point the earthly historical phenomenon of Jesus." Again the author writes, " . . . if Jesus is 'true man,' while the Christian faith asserts of him that he is the revelation in personal form of the Father—the loving God—then we are indeed bound to recognize the consequence of God's saving presence within the message and finite compass of Jesus' humanity."[220] If there is a unique universal significance for Jesus Christ, then it must be in Jesus' actual being-as-man, not behind or above it; if it is not simply ideological, something in Jesus' mode of being human, in his life and message, must point in that direction.

From an historical standpoint it is impossible to determine whether a human being bound by time and history has a universal definitive and distinctive significance for all human beings. The unique universal significance of Jesus cannot be historically demonstrated. As Schillebeeckx writes:

> Of course, the question about the unique and universal significance of Jesus is one that can only be answered in terms of belief, whether we say yes to it or no. Therefore the relevance of a positive reply is essentially theological; it cannot be simply historical. On the other hand faith-utterances must have a basis in the history of Jesus; were the opposite the case, they would have a disjunctive, thus an ideological relation to the real state of affairs. So from the historical reality that was Jesus something must have issued which people could, should and in the end were compelled by their faith to express, and rightly express, in those faith-utterances. There must have been something in the historical situation to indicate that anyone who sees Jesus has actually seen the Father. Had the gap between these two planes

been too great, Christianity would never have stood a chance. On the other hand the faith-motivated affirmation is always vulnerable in the face of the historian's conclusions. To put it another way: the unique universality of Jesus cannot be historically demonstrated either by starting from Jesus of Nazareth simply or from a systematic comparison between various world religions. What we have is an affirmation of Christian faith which claims however to be an asset to reality—although the claim to reality is in itself also an act of faith.[221]

The historical reality that was Jesus, his mode-of-being human, is the intermediary for God's salvific presence; that historical reality and that mode-of-being-human are expressed ambivalently and contingently. There simply cannot be an "idealistic" approach to Jesus' humanity. It is essential not to annihilate Jesus' human history in an overlay of cosmological myths of ideal humanity. As historical and not ideal, Jesus' humanity in its concreteness is as difficult to get at as any other human reality and possibly more so, since we are totally dependent on the historical existence and the faith of the early Church. On the basis of our historical knowledge about the life of Jesus it is impossible to establish with any real certitude the claim that Jesus was like no other man, that he is the norm for all others. The nature of the New Testament documents makes such historical assertions impossible. As D. Nineham wrote in the epilogue of *The Myth of God Incarnate:*

> The chief concern of this paper is to insure as far as possible that those who continue to make such a claim for the uniqueness of Jesus and speak, for example, of the "new humanity," "the man wholly for others," or "the man wholly for God" are fully aware of the problems involved in making and justifying any such claims. . . . It is impossible to justify any such claim on purely historical ground, however wide the net for evidence is cast.[222]

Jesus' history, his message, his mode-of-being-human as related to us in the Scriptures, and therefore through the faith of his disciples, presents itself to every generation as an invitation and a catalyzing question. What people are seeking ultimately is valid truth, the meaning and aim of life, a reason for the hope that they cannot abandon, a possibility of becoming free from suffering and death and a justification for their love of God and their fellow men and women.

4. Jesus as the Invitation and the Question

It is in his being-human-for-the-other as we see this expressed in the Scriptures that Jesus is the invitation and the question. As such an invitation and such a question, Jesus' humanity, his own mode-of-being-human, has universal significance without being exclusivistic. Jesus of Nazareth, in the concreteness of his life, relates to our on-going quest for ultimate reality. This universal significance relates to the actual on-going phenomenon of our being human. It cannot be affirmed apart from the continuing concrete effects of Jesus' history. Those effects should be visible in the practice of Christian living; the factor mediating between the historical Jesus and his significance for us now is in concrete terms the product of Christian living within our continuing human history.

As the human face of God, as an embodiment of God's salvific presence, Jesus' humanity has a unique and universal significance for all. Yet this significance is also historically mediated. The nature of history is to be real and contingent, neither absolutely one nor absolutely plural. Human history is ambiguous; a unique universal significance of any particular historical person can only be had eschatologically. As eschatological it appears as an hypothesis of which the cognitive value and so the value as reality, as truth, will have to appear from its being tested on the material of our human experience in history and ultimately in the future, from the end. In light of Jesus Christ the question of the *humanum* and therefore also of the *divinum* can only be answered by way of search and quest. That Jesus Christ is the eschatological human face of God cannot mean that the fullness of the reign of God has already come in Jesus and that subsequent history is merely a waiting for what God has accomplished, to become obvious to the eyes of unbelievers. This absolutizing of one human being, this freezing of the attention on the past, divides religions into competitive centers and makes genuine dialogue among religions impossible.

We cannot abolish the real, historical Jesus for an idealistic myth. Jesus presents himself as a man of hope and faith, one who ventured his life for the kingdom of God. His universal significance for us today does not abolish the fact that we are also in the same historical situation making our way in hope and faith. Ours is still the human project. What has already been accomplished cannot be identified with what has been promised. Faith must take the risk of the ambiguity of the historical.

In our pluralistic situation we do well to recognize the distinction between Jesus of Nazareth understood as an invitation and a catalyzing question and the Christological answer given by the Christian Churches to the fundamental question of the *humanum*. What emerges from "a below" approach is a "Christology of quest," a "catalytic Christology." We are lured into an encounter with that reality which comes historically to expression in Jesus the Christ.

As the human face of God and in his eschatological role Jesus Christ functions as a salvific symbol for the realization of his message. As Schillebeeckx writes:

> Thus Jesus of Nazareth reveals in his own person the eschatological face of all humanity and in so doing discloses the Trinitarian fullness of God's unity of being, as in its essence and in absolute freedom a gift to man. Jesus' being-as-man is "God translated" for us. His pro-existence as man is the sacrament among us of the pro-existence or self-giving of God's own being. In Jesus God has willed in his Son, and "in fashion as a man," to be God for us. The unique universality lies, therefore, in Jesus' eschatological humanity, sacrament of God's universal love for human beings.[223]

The eschatological is the realm of the symbolic. It is possible to view the symbolic as opposed to the historical. The symbolic is thought to refer to the timeless and universal and thus is indifferent and not bound up to the particular, to the historical. Its evocative powers, one may suspect, rest upon its correspondence to archetypes deeply rooted in nature itself, and not in the historical and particular event.

Yet there is a profound affinity between the symbolic and the historical because of the ambiguity of the historical itself. The historical is in need of the symbolic and no sharp line of demarcation can be made between them. To insist on the historical context for Jesus' universal and distinctive significance in no way undermines the function of the symbolic. History is never simply about historical facts; facts have a variety of depths, value, meaning. History as an interpretation of the past is not opposed to the interpretative function of the symbols. According to M. Eliade, the historical and the symbolic "represent two different modes of existence in the world, two different approaches of the mind to the interpretation of the data of reality."[224]

The historical has a transhistorical value as it affects us today in relation to fundamental questions about humanness and salvation. Symbol and history are not mutually exclusive; they need one another. To overstress the historical event over the symbol is to fall into historicism. L. Dupré sees a tendency in the Judaeo-Christian religions to overstress history: "Though history is indissolubly connected with it, salvation, if the term is to retain its meaning, must take place in the present. Christians and Jews appear to experience considerable difficulty in reconciling this present with the inherent historicity of their faiths. Often they favor the latter, regarding their faith as a new, decisive epoch of history. But in doing so, they reduce the redemption of time itself to a purely temporal event and sacrifice its basic meaning."[225]

The essential relation of Christian theology to a particular history implies that God acts differently or uniquely in certain times and places, that certain events and sections of history are for us more revelatory than others of the depths of God's divine being and the mystery of his divine purposes. For Christian theology these are uniquely unique events. Historical and philosophic analyses are not enough. Philosophy can only uncover the general pervasive and universal structure of reality. While the historical and the philosophical are necessary to Christian theology, the symbol is essential. In order to speak about God's special deed and presence in Jesus Christ one needs the realm of the symbolic.

So one must speak about Jesus Christ as symbol. Charles Davis writes about Jesus Christ "as a dynamic image, focusing the imagination, releasing the emotions, and moving to action." "He is the embodiment of meaning, expressing both the objective content of God's supreme revelation and the subjective union of man with God."[226] Jesus Christ must be spoken of as a symbolic reality.[227] To say that Jesus as the Christ, as the eschatological prophet, is a symbol is not to trivialize his historicity and his uniqueness and to reduce him to the level of a cipher for timeless and universal truths.

According to Van Harvey,[228] these objections rest on the crude juxtaposition of symbol and event that in turn rests on an unhistorical view of human nature. The distinction between timeless truths and events is too crude for theological purpose. The power of a paradigmatic event is precisely the fusion of universality and particularity. Once this principle is grasped, then symbol and history are not perceived as opposites.[229] Jesus Christ is a symbol and the events of his life and death are salvifically symbolic for all humanity precisely because of the intrinsically symbolic quality of Jesus' humanity. In an important essay written in 1959,[230] Karl Rahner has elaborated an understanding of symbol that sheds light on the question of the relationship between the historical humanity of Jesus and his symbolic function. According to Rahner the symbolic is not simply attached to persons and events. Events, persons and things do not have a symbolic quality; they *are* symbolic. "All beings are by their nature symbolic, because they necessarily express themselves in order to attain their own nature."[231] Events, persons and things are symbolic for themselves and in themselves before they are such for others.

Jesus' humanity in its own historical dimension is symbolic in itself and for us. It is the characteristic of a symbol that it speaks most directly and persuasively when it reflects the structure of our own psyche. The symbols which speak to us most meaningfully are those of which we have inner experience, those which tell us of reality by telling us of ourselves. The Christ-event as symbol is the outward expression that calls to life and feeds what is already part of our own inner disposition. It shows us what we are and thus enables us to actualize our potentialities as sons of God. This affirmation about the symbolic nature of Christ's humanity as it affects us today does not necessarily lead to what has been called an archetype Christology. Christ is not simply the "ideal" which needs to be realized in every individual. The incarnation need not be understood as the historization of an archetype which is already found at work everywhere. This kind of approach makes it impossible to focus the archetypal ideal in any unique way in a particular individual at the same time. As E. Teselle writes, "it is clear that Jesus cannot be understood solely as the fulfillment of an ideal, since he is also the proclaimer of the coming kingdom, and to it he devotes his attention, his energies and his life. Even if the original ideal is in some sense fulfilled by Jesus, the movement of human history is not slowed down when it reaches him but is, if anything, accelerated toward the realization of the kingdom in—or at least for—all people."[232] A gap remains between promise and fulfillment. Again the historical dimension of the Christ-event comes to the fore as TeSelle writes: "If Jesus can be considered unique in this 'history of salvation' in that he is experienced as 'archetype' or the new Adam, he can be called this only because he belongs fully to the human race in all its concreteness, closing the gap between the divine call and the human response—not statically, however, so that he becomes a social object, but as one who was still 'on the way' participating in and overcoming temptation, manifesting concern for his compassion, bringing the divine call fully into relation with concrete human situations."[233]

While the criterion for the truth of a symbol is existential verification, and the existential certitude of the believer lies in the finite givenness of the experiential, it cannot be totally one's subjective response that constitutes Jesus as "revelation of God," as paradigmatic event, as a symbol of mankind's unity/identity with God. Otherwise the reason for a special relationship to Jesus as the Christ would be problematic. What is it about the historical Jesus independently of any appropriation that grounds his symbolic and transforming nature? What is the nature of the "fact" of Jesus?

Different authors and lately David Tracy make a distinction between fact as actualization and fact as representation. Tracy distinguishes between two different ways that possibilities can become fact: (a) through actualization of a human possibility in human action or (b) through the representing of a possibility in a disclosive symbolic language and action. In this sense primordial symbols are not mere possibilities, but facts, not as the actualization of possibilities, but facts as rituals—as symbolic representation of a particular authentic possibility and not mere possibility.

The title Christ represents a certain possibility, not explicitly an actualization of that possibility by the one who holds the title. The question about Jesus as the Christ is "not a primary question of fact" but of "meaning and truth of the claim that Jesus is in fact the Christ; that the representation really present in the office of Messiah may be found in the words, deeds, and destiny of Jesus of Nazareth,"[234] and that the truth of human existence is re-presented "with factual finality in the singular history of Jesus of Nazareth."[235] In the affirmation of Jesus as Lord, we find the factual symbolic re-presentation of a new agapeic possibility for existence.

While the Christian community cannot disavow its own historical past, where the Christ event is the decisive one for its self-understanding, yet this cannot mean that only in and through the Christ-event has the divine been disclosed. Jesus as symbol cannot be confused with the reality he symbolizes—the presence of the universal and eternal God in human history. To say that Jesus as symbol for the Christian community is exclusive and has an overwhelming power of meaning is not the same as claiming that the reality being symbolized by Jesus as the Christ cannot be conveyed by another symbol for another tradition.

The finality and uniqueness of Jesus Christ involves a personal response; the judgment about the person of Jesus Christ is a deeply personal matter. As is true of all personal matters, it demands the freedom of faith and it is always open to an eventually deeper revelation. In the realm of symbols, questions of finality and uniqueness do not fit into finished categories, once-and-for-all realities. Rather, they imply a dynamic process and are basically developmental as faith itself.

Symbols are known by indwelling and not simply from without; they demand a participatory knowing. By engaging in symbols, by inhabiting their environment, one discovers new horizons for life, new reasons for choice and decision.

The truth of symbols, then, is not purely historical. It is relative to the degree to which the symbols offer a coherent interpretation of the whole of human experience and thereby effectively shape our thoughts, affections and actions in a constructive direction. As N.

Perrin writes about symbols, "the only kind of history by which they may be judged or validated is that of the history of an individual or people in the concrete circumstances of life in the world."[236]

6. Transymbolization

The symbolic nature of the Christ event renders a dialogical approach to other religious traditions more viable. R. Panikkar has suggested an encounter between religious traditions through the process of transymbolization. This entails the encounter of different religions on the level of their root experiences and symbols. The focus is not on specific doctrines but the complex of symbols which each tradition views as its most representative and constitutive. Yet, while insight into and understanding of another's symbol complex is possible, this complex does not open itself losely to an outsider. Religious traditions including Christianity are so deeply rooted in the texture of ordinary social existence that their symbol complex cannot but reflect the diversity of that texture. To be effective and constitutive, symbols have to be internalized. And when they are internalized they are interpreted with all the particularities of time and space that exist in the lives of the faithful. It is difficult to transfer symbols from one culture to another. Although insight and understanding into another's symbol complex is possible, this complex does not open itself easily to an outsider on the level of experience. Such experience remains ultimately unobjectifiable though not closed to a more existential encounter of faiths.

While transymbolization is a possible process, it is clear that the dialogue with other traditions cannot necessarily be based on commonality. We cannot simply assume that as we go deeply into our respective experiences we will move toward the same reality. All symbols are deeply embodied and it is different to exhort a universal essence.

Christianity has been understood as based on particular and historical symbols. The questions of uniqueness and finality have their grounds not only in the classical doctrine of the incarnation but in the New Testament itself. The adoption of a universalistic stand and a non-exclusivistic Christology demands a reinterpretation of New

Testament symbols and doctrine. Stephen Neil writes that it is inevitable that the Christian faith will

> ... cast the shadow of falsehood, or at least of imperfect truth, on every other system. This Christian claim is naturally offensive to the adherents of every other religious system. It is almost as offensive to modern man, brought up in the atmosphere of relativism, in which tolerance is regarded almost as the highest of the virtues. But we must not suppose that this claim to universal validity is something that can quietly be removed from the Gospel without changing it into something entirely different from what it is. The mission of Jesus was limited to the Jews and did not look immediately beyond them; but his life, his method and his message do not make sense, unless they are interpreted in the light of his own conviction that he was in fact the final and decisive Word of God to men. ... For the human sickness there is one specific remedy, and this is it. There is no other.[237]

7. The Authority of Scripture

One cannot deny the hermeneutical problem inherent here, nor the question posed to the authority of Scripture. Is it possible to move from one set of symbols to another without trivializing the Scriptures? Is it possible to say this while some symbols which originally expressed a revelatory event have now become dated and are no longer able to occasion a later revelatory event? Under what condition is a change of symbols called for? In this process, is the fundamental authority of the Scriptures at stake?

The normativeness of the Scriptures has been tied in the past to a supernaturalistic understanding of revelation. In this perspective the truth, claim and authority of Scripture are conceived in a-historical and dogmatic terms. In any theological questions the Scriptures function as proof text or first principle. As E. Schüssler Fiorenza writes: "On this level, the Bible often functions as ideological justification of the moral, doctrinal or institutional interests of the Church."[238]

The New Testament is an interpretation, a reading in faith. It cannot be a distillation of the sterile, germ-free content of revelation, expressed in a timeless language, valid for all ages, inspired by a timeless contemplation of the unambiguous meaning of the symbols. The Christian saving events present the same basic ambiguity as all other symbolic events: they share the polyvalence and opacity of all human history. They occur within a period of history, in a certain community, with its own characteristic culture, opinions and moods. They are experienced by men and women who bring to their involvement the totality of their own aptitudes, character, opinions, and prejudices.

Schillebeeckx has defined revelation as "an action of God as experienced by believers and interpreted in religious language and therefore expressed in human terms in the dimension of our utterly human history."[239] In this concept of revelation Scripture is seen in the full dimension of its historicity. It needs to be analyzed both historically and critically. The historical-critical method shows how interwoven the Christian faith is with its cultural, political and societal contexts, to a point that it is difficult to separate biblical revelation from its cultural expression.

The historical critical method poses the question about the canonicity of the Scriptures. While the original authority of Scripture lies in the element of revelation which has come through the experience of the early Church, the canonization represents an institutionalization. Yet, according to E. Schüssler Fiorenza, "the canon should not be viewed . . . in an exclusive fashion as a negative judgment. . . . It should be understood in an inclusive fashion as creating a pluriform model of Christian Church and Christian life."[240] A crucial issue emerges from this understanding—the issue of the "canon within the canon": How does one evaluate the various traditions that constitute the Scriptures? It has been suggested that one basic criterion for such an evaluation is salvation. As Vatican II writes: "Therefore since everything asserted by the inspired authors or social writers must be held to be asserted by the Holy Spirit, it follows that the books of Scripture must be acknowledged as teaching firmly, faithfully and without error that truth which God would put into the social writings for the sake of our salvation."[241] Karl Rahner sees this statement as leading to "an hermeneutical principle for interpreting individual texts of Scripture."[242] God's universal salvific will should be the basic criterion to evaluate other affirmations in the New Testament.

The various affirmations of the New Testament need to be interpreted in light of this basic principle. What is needed in relation to our understanding of the symbols of the new Testament that relate to Christ's uniqueness and finality is not only an understanding of their historical meaning but also a critical evaluation of their theological function in the contemporary Church.

The New Testament's claim to the uniqueness and finality of Jesus Christ comes out of a Jewish eschatological framework. It is inescapably bound up with a view of time that is linear and peculiar to the Old Testament. Yet what it means to be a Christian today differs profoundly from what it meant to be a Christian in the first generation of the Church. The present reality of faith, even the mode of existence to which we are now called, may be different from that to which the New Testament points. The historical experience of the event of Jesus is open to more than one historical interpretation. To exhibit the variety of interpretations admissible in the experience of Christian certitude is to demonstrate the falsity of the idea that the Christian already has indubitably certain answers to all matters of dispute in religion. It is only an arrogant narrow-mindedness that could imagine that a single life-experience was a sufficient basis for an interpretation of God's salvific activity in and love for all creation. As J. Cobb writes: "If we view faith as a dynamic and self-transcending force in Christian history, then indeed our understanding of our relation to the Bible is altered. Rather than seeking an essential form of faith identical with that witnessed to in the Scriptures we must seek to discern in the present the movement of the Spirit that is continuous with a movement begun in primitive Christianity."[243]

Recent approaches to the claim for Jesus' exclusive uniqueness have affirmed that this claim does not constitute the essential affirmation of the New Testament. P. Knitter writes: "In the light of recent hermeneutical studies, it can be argued that the claim for Jesus' exclusive uniqueness does not form part of the central assertion of the Christian texts, i.e., of what David Tracy, with Paul Ricoeur, calls the 'referent' of the text, its suggested 'mode-of-being-in-the-world.' "[244] The claims that this new "mode-of-being-in-the-world" "takes place only in him can be said to result from the historically conditioned world view and thought patterns of the time. Therefore these latter claims do not belong to the care of the Christian message."[245]

The task that lies ahead in the encounter with other traditions is to remain faithful to the life-giving truth of the New Testament and on the other hand seek to free ourselves from an exclusive language and concept that hinder human and Christian growth. There is a way in which the authority of the Scriptures can be reasonably affirmed without arrogance and in a non-exclusivist way. To be a Christian is to affirm one way of life rather than another; but the actual final court of appeal for determining what is the best way, the historical realm, has no grounds for exclusivity and absoluteness.

Notes

1. The term non-Christian is a Christian-centered term which defines other religions not in themselves but negatively in relation to Christianity.

2. Cf. Paul Tillich, *The Future of Religions* (N.Y.: Harper & Row, 1966); James M. Carmody, "Towards a Comparative Christology," in *Horizons* (Fall 1974), pp. 15–33; J. M. Carmody, "A Next Step for Catholic Theology," in *Theology Today* 32 (1976), pp. 371–383; Klaus Klostermaier, "A Hindu-Christian Dialogue on Truth," in *Journal of Ecumenical Studies,* Vol. 12, No. 2 (1975), pp. 157–173; Richard H. Drummond, "Christian Theology and the History of Religions," in *Journal of Ecumenical Studies,* 12 (1975), pp. 389–405.

3. Robley E. Whitson, *The Coming Convergence of World Religions* (N.Y.: Newman, 1971).

4. Cf. John S. Dunne, *The Way of All the Earth* (N.Y.: Macmillan, 1972).

5. Cf. Choan Seng Song, "The Role of Christology in the Christian Encounter with Eastern Religions," in *Christ and the Younger Churches,* ed. by Georg F. Vicedom (London: SPCK, 1972), pp. 68–83.

6. Charles Davis, *Christ and the World Religions* (N.Y.: Herder & Herder, 1971), pp. 39–44.

7. Cf. R. Ruether, *Faith and Fratricide, The Theological Roots of Anti-Semitism* (N.Y.: Seabury Press, 1974).

8. M. Wiles, "Christianity Without Incarnation?" in J. Hick, ed., *The Myth of God Incarnated* (Philadelphia: Westminster Press, 1977), p. 1.

9. *Ibid.*

10. D. N. Nineham, "Epilogue," in J. Hick, ed., *op. cit.,* p. 202.

11. J. Jeremias, *Jesus' Promise to the Nations* (London: SCM Press, 1967).

12. This is the important and influential doctrine of the *Logos spermaticos.*

13. According to Frances Young: "... that Jesus inaugurated the end of history and will consummate its goal is basic to New Testament thinking and is intimately linked with the belief that he fulfilled all the predictions of the prophets. It was rather this than a doctrine of divine incarnation which constituted the basis of the New Testament claim to finality in Jesus Christ": "The Finality of Christ," in M. Goulder, ed., *The Debate Continued: Incarnation and Myth* (Grand Rapids, Mich.: Eerdmans, 1979), p. 179.

14. G. Rupp, *Christologies and Cultures Toward a Typology of Religious World Views* (The Hague: Mouton, 1974), pp. 140–161. Cf. W.

L. Shepherd, "Hegel as a Theologian," in *Harvard Theological Review,* 41 (1968), pp. 583–603.

15. Cf. Van A. Harvey, *The Historian and the Believer* (N.Y.: Macmillan, 1965).

16. G. Rupp, *op. cit.,* p. 188.

17. D. F. Strauss, *The Life of Jesus Critically Examined,* tr. M. Evans (N.Y.: Calvin Blanchard, 1860).

18. Quoted in G. Rupp, *op. cit.,* p. 142.

19. F. Schleiermacher, *On Religion,* tr. J. Olman (N.Y.: Harper, 1958).

20. J. Macquarrie, "Kenoticism Reconsidered," in *Theology 77* (1974), p. 117.

21. W. Bousett, *Kyrios Christos: A History of the Religious Belief in Christ From the Beginnings of Christianity to Irenaeus* (Nashville: Abingdon, 1970).

22. E. Troeltsch, *Die Bedeutung Der Geschichtlichkeit Jesus für de Glauben* (Tübingen: J.C.B. Mohr-Paul Siebeck, 1911).

23. Quoted in G. Rupp, *op. cit.,* p. 222.

24. Quoted in *ibid.,* p. 223.

25. Quoted in *ibid.,* p. 225.

26. E. Troeltsch, "The Place of Christianity Among the World Religions" in *Christian Thought: Its History and Application,* ed. F. von Hugel (London: University of London Press, 1923) p. 29.

27. K. Barth, *Church Dogmatics,* I/2 (Edinburgh: T. & T. Clark) p. 1.

28. *Ibid.,* p. 329.

29. *Ibid.,* pp. 320, 335.

30. *Ibid.,* p. 369.

31. *Ibid.,* p. 487.

32. *Ibid.,* p. 490.

33. W. Pannenberg, "The Revelation of God in Jesus of Nazareth," in J. M. Robinson, ed. *Theology as History* (N.Y.: Macmillan, 1967) p. 104.

34. Cf. W. Pannenberg, *What Is Man? Contemporary Anthropology in Perspective* (Philadelphia: Fortress Press, 1972), pp. 1–14.

35. W. Pannenberg, "The Revelation of God in Jesus of Nazareth," *op. cit.,* p. 125.

36. W. Pannenberg, *Jesus—God and Man* (Philadelphia: Westminster, 1968), p. 28.

37. *Ibid.,* p. 48.

38. *Ibid.,* pp. 33–37.

39. *Ibid.,* p. 37.

40. *Ibid.,* p. 323.

41. W. Pannenberg, *Basic Questions in Theology* I (London: SCM Press, 1970), p. xvi.

42. W. Pannenberg, "The Revelation of God in Jesus of Nazareth," *op. cit.,* p. 134.

43. *Ibid.*

44. *Ibid.,* p. 142.

45. *Ibid.,* p. 143.

46. *Ibid.,* p. 133.

47. Cf. C. F. Hallencreutz, *New Approaches to Men of Other Faiths, 1938–1968. A Theological Discussion* (Research Pamphlet No. 18, WCC) (Geneva, 1970), pp. 56–62.

48. John Cobb, *Christ in a Pluralistic Age* (Philadelphia: The Westminster Press, 1975).

49. *Ibid.,* p. 63.

50. *Ibid.,* pp. 20–21.

51. *Ibid.,* p. 21.

52. *Ibid.,* p. 24.

53. *Ibid.,* p. 187.

54. "Theology knows that it must serve Christ, but it is only now learning that it does so by allowing itself to be creatively transformed by that discipline and to desacralize every form in which Christ has previously been known": *ibid.,* p. 62.

55. "Christ has been the symbol of Christian exclusive superiority whereas the word is here appealed to as identifying the principle of critical overcoming of any such exclusiveness": *ibid.,* p. 54.

56. *Ibid.,* p. 27.

57. *Ibid.*

58. J. Cobb, "A Whiteheadian Christology" in D. Brown, ed., *Process Philosophy and Christian Thought* (Indianapolis: Bobbs-Merrill, 1971).

59. *Ibid.,* p. 391.

60. "Buddhists have stressed that there is no such self-identical sub-

stance enduring through time and especially that the self born in such status Christians should agree. They should more fully appropriate the recent stress on a social self, that is, on a self that emerges out of a social matrix": John Cobb, *Christ in a Pluralistic Age, op. cit.,* p. 212.

61. *Ibid.,* p. 71.

62. *Ibid.,* p. 138.

63. *Ibid.*

64. *Ibid.,* p. 257.

65. "What is incarnate is the transcendent Logos: so it is not false to attribute to Christ the transcendent character of deity as well, but Christ as an image does not focus on deity, in abstractions from the world but as incarnate in the world—that is, as creative transformations": *ibid.,* p. 77.

66. *Ibid.,* p. 16.

67. *Ibid.,* p. 257.

68. *Ibid.,* p. 257.

69. *Ibid.,* pp. 132–138.

70. Shubert M. Ogden, *Christ Without Myth* (N.Y.: Harper & Row, 1961).

71. *Ibid.,* p. 124.

72. "To be sure, the Church stands by the claim that the decisive manifestation of this divine word is none other than the human word of Jesus of Nazareth and thence of its own authentic proclamation. But the point of this claim is not that Christ is manifest only in Jesus and nowhere else, but that the word addressed to men *everywhere,* in all events of their lives, is none other than the word spoken in Jesus and in the preaching and sacraments of the Church": *ibid.,* p. 156.

73. "Christian existence is always a 'possibility in fact' as well as a 'possibility in principle.' This may also be expressed by saying that the specific possibility of faith in Jesus Christ is one and the same with a general ontological possibility belonging to men simply as such. . . . This possibility is not man's own inalienable possession, but rather is constantly *being made possible for him* by virtue of his inescapable relation to the ultimate source of his existence. To be human means to stand *coram Deo* and, by reason of such standing, to be continually confronted with the gift and demand of authentic human existence": *ibid.,* p. 140.

74. S. Ogden, *The Reality of God* (N.Y.: Harper & Row, 1966) p. 186.

75. S. Ogden, *Christ Without Myth, op. cit.,* p. 160.

76. S. Ogden, *Reality of God, op. cit.,* p. 184.

77. *Ibid.,* p. 184.

78. A. Whitehead, *Modes of Thought* (N.Y.: The Macmillan Co., 1938), p. 52.

79. A. Whitehead, *Religion in the Making* (N.Y.: The Macmillan Co., 1926), p. 131.

80. S. Ogden, *Reality of God, op. cit.,* p. 116.

81. *Ibid.*

82. *Ibid.,* p. 69.

83. S. Ogden, "The Point of Christology," in *The Journal of Religions,* Vol. 54, No. 4 (1975), p. 392. "The task of Christology today is to elaborate the claim that Jesus is the truth of human existence made fully explicit, meaning by this claim that the possibility of faith working through love that Jesus re-presents to us through the Christian witness of faith is precisely our own authentic possibility of response to God's grace": *ibid.,* p. 393.

84. S. Ogden, *Christ Without Myth, op. cit.,* pp. 162–163.

85. S. Ogden, "The Point of Christology," *op. cit.,* p. 382.

86. "Consequently, if empirical-historical research should prove that Jesus did not in fact say or do what he is taken to have said or done, this need not the least affect the truth of what the Christian witness of faith asserts, as distinct from what it assumes. For, whatever the empirical truth of the matter, it could still be existentially true that man's only authentic possibility is the possibility that this witness takes Jesus to represent his words, deeds and tragic death": *ibid.,* p. 387.

87. "Thus, what I properly mean when I assert that Jesus is 'divine' is that the possibility here and now re-presented to me in the Christian witness of faith is God's own gift and demand to my existence. On the other hand what I properly mean when I assert that Jesus is 'human' is that I am here and now actually confronted with this possibility: that it is actually re-presented to me as an historical event and hence is not merely an idea as general truth": *ibid.,* p. 385.

88. S. Ogden, *Christ Without Myth, op. cit.,* p. 144.

89. John Hick, *God and the Universe of Faiths* (N.Y.: St. Martin's Press, 1973).

90. *Ibid.,* p. 131.

91. *Ibid.,* p. 101.

92. *Ibid.,* p. 106.

93. *Ibid.*

94. ". . . to call Jesus God, Son of God, God incarnate, etc., is to use poetic (or, if you like, mythological) language which appropriately expresses loving devotion and commitment but which is misused when it is revealed as a set of literal propositions from which to draw further literal conclusions that the imagery of incarnation has no literal meaning; this was made clear by the history of the Christological heresies, most of which were misguided attempts to give literal content to the idea of incarnation instead of leaving

it in the realm of mystery and religious myth": John Hick, "Christ's Uniqueness," in *Reform* (1974), p. 19.

95. John Hick, "Christ's Uniqueness," *op. cit.,* p. 18.

96. *Ibid.,* p. 19.

97. John Hick, *The Universe of Faith, op. cit.,* p. 152.

98. *Ibid.,* p. 152.

99. *Ibid.,* p. 153.

100. *Ibid.,* p. 174.

101. John A. T. Robinson, *The Human Face of God* (Philadelphia: The Westminster Press, 1973).

102. *Ibid.,* p. 216.

103. *Ibid.*

104. *Ibid.,* p. 220.

105. *Ibid.,* p. 229.

106. *Ibid.,* p. 203.

107. *Ibid.*

108. *Ibid.,* p. 218.

109. *Ibid.,* p. 209.

110. Paul Knitter, "European Protestant and Catholic Approaches to the World Religions: Complements and Contrasts," in *Journal of Ecumenical Studies,* Vol. 12, No. 1 (1975), pp. 13–29.

111. Cf. *Declaration on the Relationship of the Church to Non-Christian Religions (Nostra Aetate); Dogmatic Constitution on the Church (Lumen Gentium),* nn. 16–17; *Decree on the Church's Missionary Activity (Ad Gentes),* nn. 7–8; *Dogmatic Constitution on Divine Revelation (Dei Verbum),* nn. 3 and 14; *Declaration on Religious Freedom (Dignitatis Humanae),* n. 4; for the general approach to others in the spirit of the dialogue, see also *Decree on Ecumenism (Unitatis Redintegratio)* and *Pastoral Constitution on the Church in the Modern World (Gaudium et Spes).* For all these documents see Walter M. Abbott, S. J., editor, *The Documents of Vatican II* (New York: Guild Press, 1966). Finally cf. *Towards the Meeting of Religions* (Washington, D.C.: USCC, 1967), for suggestions for dialogue by the Secretariat for Non-Christians.

112. "Religions . . . are found everywhere which strive variously to answer the restless stirrings of the human heart by proposing 'ways,' consisting of teachings, rules of life, and sacred ceremonies. The Catholic Church rejects nothing which is truly and holy in these religions. It looks with sincere respect upon those ways on conduct and of life, those rules and teachings which, though differing in many particulars from what it holds and sets forth, nevertheless often reflect a ray of that Truth which enlightens every man. Indeed, it proclaims and must ever proclaim Christ, 'the Way, the

Truth and the Life,' in whom men find the fullness of religious life and in whom God has reconciled all things to himself": *Declaration on the Relationship of the Church to Non-Christian Religions,* nn.2–3.

113. A. R. Schlette, *Towards a Theology of Religions* (N.Y.: Herder & Herder, 1963), p. 17.

114. *Declaration on the Relationship of the Church to Non-Christian Religions, op. cit.*

115. This position is very much in evidence in Jean Daniélou's treatment of the relationship between Christianity and non-Christian religions: "The Church has never treated the doctrines of the pagans with contempt and disdain: rather, it has freed them from all error, then completed them and crowned them with Christian wisdom": "The Transcendence of Christianity," in *Introduction to the Great Religions* (Notre Dame: Fides, 1964), p. 155.

116. R. Latourelle writes in this regard: "In the twentieth century, under the influence of the currents of contemporary thought (existentialism, personalism), it (revelation) is the personal encounter with the living and personal God that occupies the center of attention both for theologian and simple believer. God reveals, but primarily he reveals himself; God speaks, but primarily he speaks to me. . . . There is insistence on the revealed truth, not only as proposed, but also as grasped and possessed. And in this revealed truth itself, there is less insistence on the signs, concepts, and propositions that express the mystery than on the mystery itself and the Person who reveals. There is open suspicion over a certain tendency, excessively conceptualistic, which sees revelation only as a system of propositions about God": *Theology of Revelation* (Staten Island, N.Y.: Alba House, 1966), p. 242.

117. "To my way of thinking, to answer such a question, one must first make inquiry into the nature of man as a real and necessarily historical being in his personal existence. Secondly, adhering to the official explicit revelation history of the Old and New Testaments, it should be demonstrated that this history is embedded in a salvation and revelation history that exists in humanity as a whole and is thus co-existent with the spiritual and cultural history of mankind. It is at least a Catholic view that has very clearly emerged during Vatican Council II, namely, that God's grace solicits, enlightens, supernaturally raises everyone who comes into this world, and presents him with salvation in Christ for his acceptance. This implies a supernatural history of salvation that co-exists with the history of mankind. With all this as a basis, we should be able to make it more comprehensible for modern man that, because of this universal history of revelation and salvation, there is also an official, reflective and explicit history of revelation bound by time and space, and that it reaches its climax in Jesus Christ": John H. Miller,

C.S.C. (ed.), *Vatican II: An Inter-Faith Appraisal* (Notre Dame & London: University of Notre Dame Press, 1966), pp. 601–602.

118. K. Rahner, "Membership in the Church, "in *Theological Investigations,* Vol. 2 (N.Y.: Herder & Herder, 1960), p. 3.

119. K. Rahner, "Anonymous Christianity and the Missionary Task of the Church," in *Theological Investigations,* Vol. 12 (N.Y.: Seabury Press, 1974), pp. 161–181.

120. Cf. Karl Rahner, "Anonymous Christians," in *Theological Investigations,* Vol. 6 (Baltimore: Hebrew Press, 1969), pp. 390–398; *idem,* "Atheism and Implicit Christianity," in *Theological Investigations,* Vol. 9 (N.Y.: Herder & Herder, 1972), pp. 145–165.

121. K. Rahner, "The One Christ and the Universality of Salvation," in *Theological Investigations,* Vol. XV (N.Y.: Seabury, 1979) p. 218.

122. *Ibid.,* p. 222.

123. *Ibid.*

124. *Ibid.*

125. "If we have understood these remarks on the Christian life correctly, then it is clear, as the sacraments show, that a Christian does indeed live a tangible and ecclesial life, but that the ultimately Christian thing about this life is identical with the mystery of human existence. And hence we can readily say that the ultimate and most specific thing about Christian existence consists in the fact that a Christian allows himself to fall into the mystery which we call God; that he is convinced in faith and in hope that in falling into the incomprehensible and nameless mystery of God he is really into a blessed and forgiving mystery which divinizes us; and that he also knows this on the level of reflexive consciousness and of his explicit faith, and he hopes for it explicitly, and does not just live it out in the anonymity of his actual existence. And to this extent to be a Christian is simply to be a human being, and one who also knows that this life which he is living, and which he is consciously living, can also be lived even by a person who is not a Christian explicitly and does not know in a reflexive way that he is a Christian": K. Rahner, *Foundations of Christian Faith* (N.Y.: Seabury Press, 1978), p. 430.

126. *Ibid.*

127. K. Rahner and H. Vorgrimler, *Dictionary of Theology* (N.Y.: Herder & Herder, 1965), p. 24.

128. K. Rahner, "The One Christ and the Universality of Salvation," *op. cit.,* p. 211.

129. *Ibid.,* p. 214.

130. *Ibid.,* p. 215.

131. *Ibid.,* p. 214.

132. K. Rahner, "Christianity and the Non-Christian Religions," in *Theological Investigations,* Vol. V (N.Y.: Seabury Press, 1974), p. 123.

133. "If, on the one hand, we conceive salvation as something specifically Christian, if there is no salvation apart from Christ . . . and if, on the other hand, God has really, truly and seriously intended this salvation for all men—then these two aspects cannot be reconciled in any other way than by stating that every human being is really and truly exposed to the influence of divine supernatural grace": *ibid.*

134. H. Urs von Balthasar has criticized Rahner's position because "it implies a relativization of the objective revelation of God in the biblical event and a sanctioning of the objective religious ways of other religions as ordinary and extra-ordinary ways of salvation": *Herder Kokrespondenz* 30 (1976), p. 76

135. Cf. J. B. Metz, *Faith in History and Society: Toward a Practical Fundamental Theology* (N.Y.: Seabury Press, 1980), p. 160.

136. R. Panikkar, *The Intra-Religious Dialogue* (N.Y.: Paulist Press, 1978), p. 2.

137. *Ibid.,* p. 10.

138. R. Panikkar, *Myth, Faith, and Hermeneutics* (N.Y.: Paulist Press, 1979), p. 206.

139. Raymond Panikkar, *The Unknown Christ of Hinduism* (London: Darton, Longman & Todd, 1961); *idem, Asia and Western Romance* (N.Y.: Collier Books, 1969).

140. R. Panikkar, "The Ways of West and East," in *New Dimensions in Religious Experience,* ed. George Devine (N.Y.: Alba House, 1970) p. 80.

141. "Christianity in India should not be an imported, fully-fledged and highly developed religion, but Hinduism itself converted—or Islam, or Buddhism, whatever it may be. . . . The process of conversion implies a death and resurrection, but, just as the risen Christ or the baptized person is the same as previously and yet it is a new being, likewise converted Hinduism is the true risen Hinduism, the same and yet renewed, transformed. In one word, the Church brings every true and authentic religion to its fulfillment through a process of death and resurrection which is the meaning of conversion": R. Panikkar, *The Relation of Christians to Non-Christian Surroundings,* ed. J. Neumer (London: Burns & Oates, 1967) p. 144.

142. R. Panikkar, *The Trinity and World Religions: Icon-Person-Mystery* (Bangalore: C.I.S.P.S., 1970), p. 3.

143. R. Panikkar, "The Category of Growth in Comparative Religion: A Critical Self-Examination," in *Harvard Theological Review,* Vol. 66, No. 1 (1973) p. 128.

144. R. Panikkar, *The Trinity and the Religious Experience of Man* (New York: Orbis Books, 1973), p. 54.

145. *Ibid.,* p. 51.

146. *Ibid.,* p. 53.

147. R. Panikkar, *Salvation in Christ: Concreteness and Universality* (Santa Barbara, Cal.: privately published, 1972), p. 62.

148. *Ibid.,* pp. 71–72.

149. *Ibid.,* pp. 32–33.

150. Cf. R. Panikkar, *The Unknown Christ of Hinduism, op. cit.,* p. 54.

151. R. Panikkar, *Salvation in Christ: Concreteness and Universality, op. cit.,* p. 50.

152. R. Panikkar, "Christians and So-Called 'Non-Christians,' " *Cross Currents* 22 (1972), p. 295.

153. H. Küng, *On Being a Christian* (N.Y.: Doubleday, 1978), p. 449.

154. *Ibid.,* p. 147.

155. *Ibid.,* p. 436.

156. *Ibid.,* pp. 391, 286–287.

157. *Ibid.,* p. 439.

158. *Ibid.,* p. 446.

159. *Ibid.,* p. 389.

160. *Ibid.,* p. 444.

161. *Ibid.,* p. 443.

162. *Ibid.,* p. 449.

163. *Ibid.,* cf. pp. 449ff.

164. *Ibid.,* p. 317.

165. *Ibid.,* p. 104.

166. *Ibid.,* p. 121.

167. *Ibid.,* p. 83.

168. *Ibid.,* p. 65.

169. *Ibid.,* p. 87.

170. *Ibid.,* p. 69.

171. *Ibid.;* cf. p. 265.

172. D. Tracy cautions against a too hasty conclusion about Christianity's claim of finality and uniqueness for other traditions: "For the fundamental theologian, to show that decisiveness—or, in the more classical terms, that 'finality'—more historically would demand, I believe, a dialectical analysis of Christianity in relationship to the other world religions: a task which would demand a full-fledged use of history of religions in fundamental theology and would, in the final analysis, prove a theological task whose successful completion would require a complete Christian dogmatics": *Blessed Rage for Order* (N.Y.: Seabury Press, 1975), p. 234.

173. H. Küng, *On Being a Christian, op. cit.,* pp. 97–98.

174. *Ibid.,* p. 426

175. *Ibid.,* p. 91.

176. *Ibid.*, p. 113.

177. *Ibid.*, p. 447.

178. Some basic classifications of theology and Christology can be found in H. Richard Niebuhr, *Christ and Culture* (N.Y.: Harper Brothers, 1967); C. Davis, *Christ and the World Religions* (N.Y.: Herder & Herder, 1971); D. Tracy, *Blessed Rage for Order. The New Pluralism in Theology* (N.Y.: Seabury Press, 1975).

179. E. O. James, *Christianity and Other Religions* (London, 1968), p. 173.

180. Cf. E. TeSelle, *Christ in Context. Divine Purpose and Human Possibility* (Philadelphia: Fortress Press, 1975), pp. 7–47.

181. John Cobb, *op. cit.*, p. 76.

182. For a different understanding cf. J. Dewart, "Christological Particularity: Need It Be a Scandal?" in *ATR*, Vol. LXII, No. 1 (1980), pp. 64–74.

183. G. Rupp, *Christologies and Cultures. Toward a Typology of Religious World Views* (The Hague: Mouton, 1974).

184. *Ibid.*, p. 199.

185. *Ibid.*, p. 200.

186. *Ibid.*, p. 4.

187. This is clearly in opposition to W. Pannenberg's position. Cf. *Jesus—God and Man* (Philadelphia: The Westminster Press, 1968), pp. 47–53.

188. G. Rupp, *op. cit.*, p. 3.

189. The realist and nominalist variables are derived from the medieval debate about the status of universals: whether universals exist extramentally or whether only individuals exist. The transactional processive variables relate to the dimension of history: a static developmental comment of history.

190. G. Rupp, *op. cit.*, p. 203.

191. *Ibid.*, p. 47.

192. *Ibid.*, p. 188.

193. P. Schineller, "Christ and Church: A Spectrum of Views," in *Theological Studies*, Vol. 37, No. 4, (1976), pp. 545–567.

194. *Ibid.*, p. 557.

195. Troeltsch arrived at his conclusion about Jesus' uniqueness through a comparative study. See his *The Absoluteness of Christianity and the History of Religions* (Richmond: John Knox, 1971).

196. Such a position is formed in E. TeSelle: "The humanity of Jesus, although it is shaped by and attests to the Word, neither exhausts the Word nor is the sole means of access to it, for the Word is both knowable and efficacious elsewhere. The uniqueness of Jesus—a uniqueness which should not be seen apart from the uniqueness of Israel and the Church—will consist

then in being the touchstone by which other responses are judged, the achievement by which their deficiencies are overcome, the center of gravity around which they cluster": *op. cit.,* p. 164.

197. Don Cupitt, "The Finality of Christ," *Theology,* Vol. 78, No. 666 (1975), p. 625.

198. *Ibid.*

199. Don Cupitt, "One Jesus, Many Christs?" in *Christ, Faith and History,* ed. S. W. Sykes (London: Cambridge University Press, 1972) p. 143.

200. *Ibid.*

201. D. Cupitt, "The Finality of Christ," *op. cit.,* p. 626.

202. Don Cupitt, "One Jesus, Many Christs?" *op. cit.,* p. 144.

203. J. Moltmann, "The Church in the Power of the Spirit" (N.Y.: Seabury Press, 1977), p. 159.

204. J. Macquarrie, "Christianity and Other Faiths," *Union Seminary Quarterly Review* 20 (1964), p. 39.

205. G. John Macquarrie, "Some Problems of Modern Christology" in *The Indian Journal of Theology,* Vol. 23 (1974), pp. 155–175.

206. D. Tracy, *Blessed Rage for Order* (N.Y.: Seabury Press, 1975), p. 206.

207. H. U. Von Balthasar, *Word and Redemption* (N.Y.: Herder & Herder, 1969), pp. 23–48.

208. Cf. A. Roper, *The Anonymous Christian* (N.Y.: Sheed & Ward, 1966).

209. Cf. V. Mann, *Theogonishe Tage* (Stuttgart, 1970).

210. Cf. W. Pannenberg, *Jesus—God and Man* (Philadelphia: The Westminster Press, 1968), pp. 47–53.

211. D. Cupitt, "One Jesus, Many Christs" in *Christ, Faith and History, op. cit.,* pp. 131–147.

212. W. Pannenberg, *op. cit.,* p. 33.

213. K. Rahner, "The Two Basic Types of Christology," *Theological Investigations* XIII (N.Y.: Seabury Press, 1975), p. 216.

214. *Ibid.,* p. 217.

215. J. Macquarrie, "Kenoticism Reconsidered," *Theology* 77 (1974), p. 121.

216. W. Pannenberg, *op. cit.,* p. 279. For a criticism of this position, cf. J. Moltmann, *op. cit.,* pp. 87–92.

217. K. Rahner, *op. cit.,* p. 215.

218. *Ibid.,* p. 216.

219. E. Schillebeeckx, *Jesus—An Experiment in Christology* (N.Y. Seabury Press, 1979) p. 604.

220. *Ibid.,* p. 635.

221. *Ibid.,* p. 604.

222. J. Hick, ed., *The Truth of God Incarnate* (Philadelphia: Westminster, 1977), pp. 194–195.

223. E. Schillebeeckx, *op. cit.,* p. 670.

224. W. L. Beane and W. G. Doty, *Myths, Rites, Symbols: A Mircea Eliade Reader* (N.Y.: Harper & Row, 1974), p. 120.

225. L. Dupré, *Transcendent Selfhood* (N.Y.: Seabury Press, 1976), p. 77.

226. Charles Davis, *Christ and the World Religions* (N.Y.: Herder & Herder, 1971), p. 124.

227. P. Knitter writes: "From differing approaches and with different terms theologians are speaking of Christ as a mythic-reality which originates from, and is continuously related to, Jesus but which cannot be identified with or limited to Jesus. This is what Tillich is about in his understanding of 'the symbol of Christ' which is an historical symbol mediating the presence of New Being; yet the symbol-creating activity of New Being cannot be limited to Jesus. Macquarrie argues and speaks of Jesus Christ as the 'symbol of Being' and the 'focusing' of the universal, saving power of Being. Much of process Christology works with the concept of the symbol: John Cobb, in his description of Christ as the universally active power of 'creative transformation,' distinguished from Jesus as the incarnation of that transformation; William N. Pittenger, with his insistence that Jesus is different in degree but not in essence from other incarnations and manifestations of universal divine Creative Love. Shubert M. Ogden is even more explicit with his forceful argument that 'the point of Christology' is 'strictly existential': what is primarily important is not what actually happened in the life of Jesus but the ability of the message (the symbol-myth) to reveal and transform our lives. Tracy follows this same line in his outline of a foundational Christology": "Jesus-Buddha-Krishna: Still Present?" in *Journal of Ecumenical Studies,* Vol. 16, No. 4 (1979), p. 660.

228. Van A. Harvey, *The Historian and the Believer* (N.Y.: Macmillan, 1966) p. 286.

229. This is affirmed by H. R. Niebuhr: "For history may function as myth or as symbol when men use it (or are forced by processes in their history itself to employ it) for understanding their present and their future. When we grasp our present, not so much as a product of our past, but more as essentially revealed in that past, then the historical account is necessarily symbolic; it is not merely descriptive of what was once the case": *The Responsible Self* (N.Y.: Harper & Row, 1963) p. 156.

230. K. Rahner, "The Theology of the Symbol" in *Theological Investigations,* Vol. 4, pp. 221–252.

231. *Ibid.,* p. 224.

232. E. TeSelle, *Christ in Context, Divine Purpose and Human Possibility* (Philadelphia: Fortress Press, 1975), p. 123.

233. *Ibid.,* p. 167.

234. D. Tracy, *Blessed Rage for Order* (N.Y.: Seabury Press, 1975), p. 211.

235. *Ibid.,* p. 217.

236. N. Perrin, *The New Testament: An Introduction* (N.Y.: Harcourt Brace, 1974), p. 29.

237. S. Neill, *Christian Faith and Other Faiths* (London: 1961), p. 166.

238. E. Schüssler Fiorenza, "For the Sake of Our Salvation . . . Biblical Interpretation or Theological Task," in D. Durken, ed., *Sin, Salvation and the Spirit* (Collegeville: Liturgical Press, 1979), p. 23.

239. E. Schillebeeckx, *Christ, the Experience of Jesus as Lord* (N.Y.: Seabury Press, 1980), p. 78.

240. E. Schüssler Fiorenza. *op. cit,* p. 23.

241. Constitution *Dei Verbum,* in W. Abbott and J. Gallagher (eds.), *The Documents of Vatican II* (N.Y.: America Press, 1966), p. 119.

242. K. Rahner, *Foundations of Christian Faith* (N.Y.: Seabury Press, 1978), p. 376.

243. J. Cobb, "The Authority of the Bible," in J. Courtney, ed., *Hermeneutics and the Worldliness of Faith* (1974), p. 201.

244. P. Knitter, *op. cit.,* pp. 153–154.

245. *Ibid.,* p. 155.